SHOP COOK EAT NEW YORK

SHOP COOK EAT NEW YORK

SUSAN MEISEL
NATHALIE SANN

RIZZOLI
NEW YORK

New York · Paris · London · Milan

First published in the
United States of America in 2016 by
Rizzoli International Publications, Inc.
300 Park Avenue South
New York, NY 10010
www.rizzoliusa.com

Recipe, page 120 [Gâteau de Crêpes]:
© 2005 Amanda Hesser, from
The New York Times. Reprinted by
permission.

2016 2017 2018 2019 / 10 9 8 7 6 5 4 3 2 1

Distributed in the U.S. trade by
Random House, New York

Printed in China

ISBN-13: 978-0-8478-4864-5

Library of Congress Catalog Control
Number: 2016939424

ACKNOWLEDGMENTS

We would like give a special thanks to our publisher, Charles Miers, who once again has had faith in our book idea; to Chris Steighner, our editor, who has been so supportive and helped us through this journey; and to Patricia Fabricant, who is responsible for the book's design. This book would not have been possible without all the shop owners who shared their personal stories and let us taste all the delicious things we wrote about. Special thanks to Christian Diaz, who made the pictures look so beautiful, Catherine Bitan and Raïssa Kouègbé, our friends who helped with the research, and Kim Fennebresque, for his editorial support.

Cooking and testing is a collaborative act and we would like to thank Lucien Sann, who gave us his eloquent opinion on each product and recipe.

I dedicate this book to my grandchildren
Benjamin, Chloe, Lucas, and Sebastien,
who always make me smile.

—Susan Meisel

To my son, the most trusted
food critic I have ever met,
and Kim Fennebresque,
for his advice and encouragement.

—Nathalie Sann

INTRODUCTION

This is our most recent journey through the streets of the five boroughs of New York on an unending quest for hidden treasures: artisans, food purveyors, and unique products.

And while creating books was the purpose of our journey, the results have far surpassed the original intent. We have seen parts of Manhattan, Brooklyn, Queens, Staten Island, and the Bronx that lifetime residents have never seen or imagined. We have met people who are the best (perhaps the best anywhere) at what they do. And while they may have achieved neither notoriety nor wealth, they have derived enormous satisfaction from their pursuit and achievement of unmatched excellence. It has been a pleasure—indeed, a privilege—for Susan and me to have had access to these extraordinary craftspeople in the food industry.

For me, I have had a chance to see New York City as few others have the chance to. And I have witnessed the shift in New York's small business and food culture: Chinatown is no longer Chinese. Eataly arrived five years ago and is now a mecca for people who love not only the food they are eating but the atmosphere the food has created. Food consumers are far more educated, and interested, in all aspects of food than they were ten years ago. No longer satisfied with grabbing food labeled as "fresh" off the grocery shelf, today's buyers want far more information: where does the food come from and how was it made? Health considerations have taken on greater importance, far more than just buying organic. Food is now fun.

It is fun to talk about: it is a common topic at dinner tables, when families and friends gather for large meals. It is fun to talk about celebrity chefs. It is fun to learn about the stories surrounding new foods emerging in the markets and in the communities.

And in the years since we wrote our first book, *Gourmet Shops of New York*, there have been changes in the food landscape that have had profound effects on all the participants in the industry. Cheese has become the talk of the town for chefs of all types and skill levels; Beecher's is a cheese maker like no other. Through a huge glass window, it is possible to see them actually making the cheese in big troughs. You can get an education in cheese making right in the middle of Manhattan.

Several butchers have created their own butchery schools and the result is that the skill has been embraced by a whole new generation of meat cutters, both male and female, who are providing better meat than ever. Union Square, as one might expect, was the site for the beginning of an ever-expanding trend, the farmers' market. Professional and home chefs come to the market to buy fresh produce brought from all over the northeast. It has afforded a better living to many farmers and access to stunningly high-quality, farm-fresh products. And what we call the hyper-niche market has gained traction in many areas. Melt, a store that specializes in ice cream sandwiches, has been a culinary and commercial success. And Dough, which makes doughnuts only, has opened its second store. Their doughnuts, incidentally, are definitely the best in New York, probably the best in America, and possibly the best in the world.

Sadly, there have been negative developments as well—principal among them has been the disappearance of many of the great family-owned and -operated stores. Rents have skyrocketed or the buildings have been sold for development. It is not our place to make political commentary on this dynamic, but the absence of these mom-and-pop establishments is a tragedy for those who patronized them and the neighborhoods that housed them. Food has that effect on neighborhoods: great food emporia attract people to neighborhoods and then those neighborhoods in turn attract new food entrepreneurs. It is a phenomenon not unlike that evidenced by the gentrification of neighborhoods by artists throughout the city. Food has become that important.

Producing a book such as *Shop Cook Eat* requires total commitment to discovering the unknown. Above all else, this is an adventure. Our partnership has been a near-perfect melding of skills and interests enhanced by a wonderfully enduring friendship. We bring our own perspectives to our subjects but retain our abiding devotion to the subject matter. Susan is an exceptional photographer who truly knows old New York. There is no part of New York that is new to her; parts may have changed, in some cases drastically, but they are not new. For me, all of New York is new; I moved here from Paris fifteen years ago and I have been exploring nonstop since I stepped off the plane. Our divergent histories in this city have enriched the experience for both of us. Having a successful catering business, Susan brings deep experience and understanding of all issues related to the food industry, and she is a great cook. I love the research part of our mission; I am constantly scouring the Internet and talking to merchants, avid cooks, and restaurateurs in the hopes of uncovering undiscovered gems for the purpose of the book, or for my clients, trying to source for them the best of the best. Like Susan, I am an experienced cook, having been trained by my family and at the French Culinary Institute in New York City. I even experienced the joy of being co-owner of Farm Candy, an artisanal company mixing salt and sugar to create unique flavors. What I enjoy most is learning about the process involved in the work done by the subjects in our book; I am

fascinated by how products are made and the skills required in the effort.

The actual creation of the book follows a formula that we have employed on each of our endeavors. The day starts with Susan fetching me in her pickup truck and then following a route that I have established the night before. That route is designed to allow us to see efficiently as many as ten (and sometimes more) businesses. We never tell the owners that we are coming, preferring to arrive unannounced. As our calling card, we bring a copy of *Gourmet Shops of New York*, in an attempt to establish our food acumen. It seems to work. Susan immediately begins to determine what sort of pictures could be taken. Her objective is to capture the nature of the producers, the atmosphere of the store, and, in many cases, the feel of the neighborhood. The neighborhood is critical to the world of food; depicting it for our readers—in words and photographs—is a very high priority for us. While Susan is busy with her camera, I am engaging the owner, workers, and customers to seek the accurate narrative of the enterprise. Since many of the shops are family owned, there is inevitably a compelling story of how the business was founded, the struggles of the early years, and the dedication to creating something special for customers.

—Nathalie Sann

CHINATOWN

As Little Italy shrinks, Chinatown is expanding east, south, and north, growing with all the excitement of a thriving immigrant community. This is the biggest Chinatown in the United States; the streets teem with vendors selling fruits, fish, toys, and umbrellas while trucks roll by loaded with cargo—baskets of shellfish, whole butchered pigs, crate after crate of the freshest vegetables. Every inch of Chinatown's sidewalks and floor space is occupied by commerce, and most of this commerce is food related. Streets once exclusively Italian are now 100 percent Cantonese. But as Lou Di Palo, the well-known Broome Street salumeria owner explains, the Chinese have nurtured the heart and the soul of Little Italy with their passion, enthusiasm, and love for good food.

Food fuels the frantic energy of Chinatown. And its stores represent almost every region of China. From the well-known cuisines like Szechuan and Hunan, full of fire and spice, to more obscure traditions such as Jiangsu and Anhui, slow cooking from the mountain regions, and Hubei, with its almost Japanese emphasis on presentation, a visit to Chinatown is a lesson in food, geography, and culture. Be sure to arrive hungry.

ASIA MARKET CORPORATION

If you've ever tried a recipe from a Southeast Asian cookbook but were stopped short by the challenge of finding kaichi, taro, and lemongrass at your local grocery store, this market will supply these ingredients and more. The Asia Market Corporation specializes in Thai, Indonesian, and Filipino products. It's a great place to expand your culinary horizons, so bring your cookbook and browse the aisles. Happily, the products are labeled in English. The selection of Asian fruits and vegetables is comprehensive, as is the selection of fresh and dried herbs and spices, which include watercress, cilantro, dried chile, fresh turmeric, coriander, and caraway. The next time a recipe calls for fresh coconut milk, you'll be able to reach into your freezer for the quart you found at Asia Market. **2**

AJI ICHIBAN

It would be easy to dismiss Aji Ichiban—a Hong Kong chain with more than ninety snack shops worldwide—as an Asian 7-11. But take a closer look and you'll pick up the delightful differences, from the sign at the door that encourages tasting to the beautiful displays and packaging (all with English translations) to the vast selection of Asian treats. One side of the store is dedicated to salty snacks like dried fish, wasabi peas, and melon seeds. On the sweet side there's peanut nougat, dried plums, cola bottle gummies, and more. Try the tasty ten-scented olives, mixed with an unusual blend of ten spices, or haikkaido squid chips. The black currant gummies are outstanding. **1**

CANTON NOODLE CORPORATION

Canton Noodle Corporation is on Mott Street in Little Italy, a neighborhood that once was a mecca for Italian immigrants and the foods they brought with them from the old country. Although you can still buy great Italian cheeses, meats, and pastries there (see Little Italy, page 51, for details), the neighborhood is predominantly Chinese. If you walk too quickly past a nondescript metal door, you will miss the wonders of the Canton Noodle Corporation, where traditional Chinese noodle making has been practiced by the Eng family for more than forty years. As we entered the store, we met one of the Eng daughters, who promptly stated, "No pictures," with a friendly smile. "Everyone wants to take pictures," she explained with good humor, and why wouldn't they? Bags of flour are piled high everywhere. The machinery, which looks similar to an Italian pasta maker, produces a variety of Chinese noodles all day. Come early in the morning and watch as hundreds of pounds of noodles appear right before your eyes. Choose from dried, egg, Shanghai, skinny, and wide noodles, as well as wonton wrappers and egg roll skins. Noodles have been a Chinese staple for centuries and Canton Noodle is carrying on that tradition in a big (and tasty) way. **3**

GOLDEN PROFIT TRADING

In Chinatown, there are many stores like Golden Profit Trading that specialize in dried seafood and medicinal herbs, but this one boasts an especially extensive and unusual array of dried goods. The use of dried herbs, spices, and other dried foods dates back to a time when there wasn't any refrigeration, and has been popular in the Asian community ever since for both their culinary and medicinal properties. Despite these foods' old appearance, they are actually quite delicious once you understand what they are and how to prepare them. You'll first notice the piles of dried shrimp, squid, oysters, mushrooms, sea cucumber, snails, and other curious items. And then you'll see the jars of peanuts, ginger, peppercorns, curry powder, curry leaves, and chiles, among many other items. You will exit this store with your purchases in a ubiquitous red plastic bag and a friendly smile from the owner and her son. **4**

GREAT PRODUCE STORES OF CHINATOWN

On a short stretch of East Broadway between Catherine and Allen Streets, you'll find several extraordinary food stalls. Also, on Bayard Street, there is Hung Lee Co., where the fruits and vegetables are pampered, spritzed, and polished hourly. The displays are meticulously ordered, and every item is sold at its peak. You won't find a single wilted lettuce leaf in this store, and you won't need to check the tomatoes for ripeness. Obsessive? Compulsive? Maybe, but the fruits and vegetables are always perfect. Among the other outstanding spots for fruits and vegetables are Lou Cheng Market, New Lung Hing Market, and Number One Long Hing Market. Chinatown is a place to wander, explore, and discover, so use your nose, your eyes, and your cook's sixth sense, and you're sure to find some great shops. **5**

LUNG MOON BAKERY

Lung Moon Bakery opened several decades ago, and the decor remains unchanged. The bakery is tiny, with low ceilings and fluorescent lights, and the walls are filled with signs wishing patrons good luck and lots of Chinese artifacts prophesying good fortune. As you enter you might wonder why this shop is so crowded with locals; the key is the kitchen in the back that produces tasty Chinese treats throughout the day. Try the egg tart in the aluminum tin, which tastes like a combination of English custard and the Portuguese egg tart pastry known as *pastéis de nata*. It turns out the Portuguese introduced this tart to Hong Kong and later to China. The recipe was then remixed by the English and became one of the most popular desserts in Asia. Lung Moon's angel cake, a variation on the sponge cake, is also delicious, as are the savory steamed meat and vegetable buns. This establishment is cash only. **6**

MARK'S WINE & SPIRITS

Located in the heart of Chinatown on Mott Street, Mark's Wine & Spirits is owned by the Woo family—they've been in business for more than seventy-five years. The spirited owner, Peter, runs the establishment with his wife, who speaks little English and remains behind the counter, but acknowledges repeat customers by name. China has a long tradition of producing wines and spirits, tracing back four thousand years. When the Woos immigrated to America, it made sense to open a liquor store in Chinatown. If you are unfamiliar with Asian wines, most of them are available in nips. Andrew, the Woo's charming grandson, will help you pair any Chinese dish with the right barley alcohol, rice wine, or plum wine. Or explore potent Chinese liquors, called *baijiu*, like Luzhu Laojiao, which dates back to the Ming Dynasty; Yanghe Daqu, which comes in three different alcohol contents; and the famous Maotai, China's official "National Liquor" and the country's most expensive domestic spirit. All labels are in Chinese but most of them have English translations. And Andrew is happy to answer questions. It looks like the Woo family will run the business for many generations to come.

If you have a hangover after sampling all these new discoveries, you can try a neck massage on Pell Street. Still not convinced? Stop at the Lin Sister Herb Shop on Bowery for one of their special hair-of-the-dog concoctions. **7**

6

7

MULBERRY MEAT MARKET

At lunchtime, Mulberry Meat Market is invaded by an army of hungry workers who head for the steam tables of prepared foods, which are extremely cheap and good. You may want to wander over to the giant counter to pick up some of the fresh and marinated meat, ready to be cooked at home. Try the flank steak or the marinated chicken in spicy sauce. The refrigerator at the back of the store displays chickens and Chinese sausages, as well as more exotic meats. **8**

NEW BEEF KING

Jerky—thin strips of marinated dried meat—was a staple of the Wild West. If a cowboy wasn't chewing tobacco, he'd be masticating a hunk of beef jerky. The word *jerky* comes from Quechua, a Native American language, so it was a bit surprising to find a beef jerky shop in Chinatown. As it turns out, just about every carnivorous culture has its own form of jerky. At New Beef King, Robert Yee makes jerky that is far more tender and juicy than the stringy, salty, jaw-wrenching American variety. Yee learned his distinctive jerky-drying technique from a great-aunt in Hong Kong. Instead of conventional dehydration, Yee painstakingly bakes the jerky by moving it from one oven to another, set at increasingly higher temperatures. In addition to the beef version, Yee makes ostrich and pork jerky. In any form, his jerky is a tasty and all-protein replacement for high-carb snacks. **9**

NEW KAM MAN

In Chinatown, they call Dean & DeLuca the "Kam Man of Soho." This two-story Chinese supermarket and kitchenware store is a one-stop immersion course in Chinese cuisine. A first visit can be daunting, but it's worth taking the time to study everything and ask a lot of questions. As you step inside Kam Man (in operation since the seventies, but more recently dubbed New Kam Man), you'll see Chinese signs everywhere; some have English translations, which make it a bit easier to explore the store. Take the leap and buy a few items that catch your eye. Much of the food here will be new to uninitiated Westerners. Barrels and trays of pungent dried fish, sea cucumber, and various dried fungi stand at the center of the store. You'll see row upon row of sauces—at least fifteen different soys, plus hoisin, oyster, five-spice, and twenty varieties of sesame oil. Try the soft drinks in their unique bottles, stoppered with glass marbles. You may prefer the taste of kamune lychee with Mountain Dew or PowerAde. At the back of the store, choose from a dozen varieties of fresh noodles, sticky rice dumplings, and fifty-pound bags of basmati or sticky rice.

New Kan Man also stocks the most complete selection of Chinese cookware in New York, including woks of all sizes, with and without handles, nonstick and preseasoned. Experiment with new cooking implements—the long, flat spoons and ladles used for stir-frying, lethal-looking cleavers, chopping blocks, steamers, and rice cookers. There's an herbalist who sells the herbs and spices used in Chinese medicine, too. Before you leave, you might as well join the line for a serving of freshly roasted duck or squid. **10**

NEW YORK MART

Incredibly, the fourth floor of this building at 128 Mott Street, which houses one of the biggest food markets in Chinatown on its ground floor, was famous for hosting a key scene in *The Godfather*. The neighborhood's large Cantonese community flocks to this supermarket from early morning until dusk to buy some of the best food staples in Chinatown. It's extremely crowded with Chinatown residents and visitors from all over, but don't be put off. The store is well organized, and even if you aren't there to buy the assortment of fruits and vegetables and cooked duck, pork, and chicken hanging from hooks, it's a feast for the eyes. The store is enormous and divided in two. The fruits, vegetables, fish, and meat are in one section; this leads to the canned and packaged foods section. The assortment of familiar items is just about as interesting as the unusual groceries. The fascinating selection of vegetables and herbs could turn anyone into a Chinese chef (or at least a wannabe chef). Equally interesting is the fish: there are live eels, catfish, fresh shrimp, red snapper, flounder, and cod, and you can also buy live frogs. While passing through the butcher department you will spy fresh-roasted poultry and meat along with other prepared dishes. The grocery department is chock-full of bottled sauces, canned vegetables, and fifty-pound bags of rice. Between the two sections a café offers an array of prepared foods. Try to find a table to take in the scene, but be prepared to wait in line to pay. **11**

SUN'S ORGANIC GARDEN

For much of human history, herbalists have been an essential part of the healing traditions around the world. But despite the many new tea brands on the market these days—Kusmi, Harney & Sons, Plain-T, Forté, and many more—few of us seem to remember that there was a time when herbs and teas were prepared as medicine to treat physical ailments. Lorna Lai, the owner of Sun's Organic Garden, is a healer who spends as much time as necessary with her customers to get a full picture of their health. She sells the tea and herb mixes she has been perfecting for years by the ounce. They are as tasty as they are salubrious for you, and she has many loyal clients.

On display in the shop are large glass jars filled to the brim with strange-looking teas with unusual names that might give you pause. But each tea is clearly explained on the jar's label. Special blends help with a range of maladies, from high cholesterol to insomnia, colds, athlete's foot, hair loss, and sexual problems. There are even tea blends for weight loss. **12**

TEN REN TEA

Two walls of this narrow shop are covered floor to ceiling with beautiful tin canisters filled with different varieties of teas and herbs. You'll find green, jasmine, and oolong teas, as well as king's tea, which is oolong blended with ginseng and which comes in green and dark varieties. There's the traditional black tea and mountain-grown white tea, which has a high concentration of purportedly health-supportive polyphenols. There's Pou Chong, a fermented green tea, Pu Erh, a dark fermented tea, and Ti Kuan Yin, an earthy postfermented Chinese tea.

That list hardly scratches the surface. This is the place to learn everything about tea, and the people behind the counter are more than willing to explain their wares. The teas come loose or in bags, depending upon your preference. Ten Ren also carries a large selection of ginseng in tea bags, as a powder, and as raw roots in capsule form. The health benefits of ginseng may be up for debate, but that doesn't seem to matter to the customers, who line up nine deep to make purchases at the store's ginseng counter. **13**

WIN SEA FOOD MARKET

From early morning to late evening, this Chinatown fish store is packed with customers, fishmongers, and deliverymen. Win Sea Food Market restocks two or three times a day, making this the place to buy the freshest fish in Chinatown. The selection is dazzling. If a species lives anywhere near water, there is a good chance you'll find it on display here: octopus, squid, salmon, trout, striped bass, sole, flounder, and porgy, available whole or filleted. The array of shellfish is impressive: oysters, sand snails, hornshells, hen and sand clams, mussels, razor clams, and the more conventional littleneck and cherrystone clams. You will also find crayfish and lobster, shelled and unshelled, cooked and uncooked; live tiger prawns, yellow shrimp, white prawns, and, in season, soft-shell crabs. The fishmongers speak English and will explain the well-arranged displays—crustaceans to the right, fish in the middle, mollusks on the left, and toads under the counter. **14**

VEGETARIAN TOFU SALAD

This recipe is from May Wong Trent, a cookbook author and food writer with an extensive repertoire of Asian recipes.

SERVES 4

FOR THE SALAD

2 cups shredded firm tofu

2-egg thin omelet, thinly sliced

2 cups canned bamboo shoots, drained and thinly sliced

1 cup canned straw mushrooms, drained and halved

½ cup fresh cilantro leaves, coarsely chopped

¼ cup scallions, green and white parts, thinly sliced

FOR THE SALAD DRESSING

⅓ cup soy sauce

1 tablespoon sesame oil

2 tablespoons vegetable oil

1 teaspoon grated fresh ginger

1 teaspoon honey or pinch sugar

Juice of ½ lemon

Salt and freshly ground black pepper

2 cups shredded iceberg lettuce

1 In a large bowl, toss together the tofu, omelet, bamboo shoots, straw mushrooms, cilantro, and scallions.

2 In a small bowl, whisk together the soy sauce, sesame oil, vegetable oil, ginger, honey, lemon juice, and salt and pepper to taste. Add to the tofu salad and toss to combine.

3 On a large plate, arrange a bed of the shredded lettuce and top with the tofu salad.

4 Serve at room temperature, over cooked noodles, or in a wrap.

STIR-FRIED SHRIMP

Win Sea Food Market

SERVES 4

This is a perfect dish for a busy home cook. It should not take more than 20 minutes to prepare and it's easy to make. The combination of the lemon juice and soy sauce will brighten this recipe.

1 (1-inch) piece fresh ginger, peeled and finely grated

2 cloves garlic, minced

2 tablespoons soy sauce

1 tablespoon canola oil

20 ounces uncooked shrimp, peeled and deveined

1 pound baby bok choy, halved lengthwise

2 ribs celery, diced

1 cup unsalted raw cashews

Salt and freshly ground black pepper

Juice of 2 lemons

Steamed white rice, for serving

1 In a small bowl, stir together the ginger, garlic, and soy sauce.

2 Heat the oil in a wok or nonstick frying pan over high heat. Add the shrimp and cook, stirring continuously, for 2 minutes. Add the baby bok choy and celery and cook, stirring occasionally, for 2 to 3 minutes until the baby bok choy turns bright green but still has some crunch. Add the ginger dressing and cashews, season with salt and pepper, and return to the heat for 1 minute more.

3 Remove the pan from the heat and stir in the lemon juice. Serve with steamed rice.

EAST VILLAGE

The East Village, the area from Fourteenth Street to Houston between Third Avenue and the East River, is the only part of the city where the avenues are designated by single letters: Avenues A, B, C, and D. In the 1970s and '80s, the East Village was so tough, locals said the D in the Avenue D was short for "dead." But all that's changed, and in the opinions of many of the old-line bohemians, the area has been homogenized beyond recognition; for those of us who did not experience the chaos of the early years, the neighborhood still retains something of a rough-edged charm.

In the late eighteenth century, new waves of immigration turned the East Village, once home to New York's largest German community, into an outpost of eastern Europe. This mélange of Polish, Ukrainian, Czech, and Russian immigrants was joined by a small cadre of Italians and eastern European Jews. As each group arrived, they unpacked their traditional foods and recipes. Later, in the 1940s and '50s, the eastern Europeans were joined by immigrants from Puerto Rico, the Dominican Republic, and Colombia, adding additional spice to the mix. In the 1960s, there was a brief psychedelic flash—enter the hash brownie—as Jimi Hendrix, Jefferson Airplane, and the Grateful Dead lit up Fillmore East. Over the past thirty years, the neighborhood has been changing again as droves of uptown types stream downtown into Alphabet City, turning rent-stabilized tenements into uptown-worthy co-ops and condos. Now old-school butchers, bakers, and pierogi makers stand side by side with new boutique bakers, chocolatiers, and craft beer stores—traditional meeting trendy in a rich culinary landscape.

BOND STREET CHOCOLATE

Lynda Stern opened this cozy shop in 2009. Her spiritual side plays out in the chocolates she designs, which include chocolate Buddhas dusted with edible 24-carat gold; figures of Ganesh, the elephant-headed Hindu deity; Jesus; as well as the Virgin of Guadalupe. The individual chocolate pieces are beautifully displayed in a glass case, like gems in a jewelry store. It's hard to resist a box of her boozy ganache bonbons infused with bourbon, tequila, and elderflower liqueur, among other flavors. Chocolate skulls inspired by Keith Richards fill round silver boxes, and the milk chocolate bar with caramelized almonds and sea salt makes the term *candy bar* feel like an epiphany. No guilt here, though: Religion, in the form of chocolate, is alive and well on Bond Street. **1**

EAST VILLAGE MEAT MARKET

This is probably the last smokehouse in Manhattan. Most of the customers speak Russian or Ukrainian, but as the neighborhood changes, more and more non-Slav New Yorkers are discovering this shop. Five butchers serve up pork sausages and superb cuts of fresh pork: pork loin, pork roast, and thinly filleted pork schnitzel. Loop upon loop of kielbasa, beer sausage, and garlic sausage festoon the racks in the smoking room and in the temperature- and humidity-controlled drying room. **2**

BAKED BREADED CHICKEN BREASTS

East Village Meat Market

SERVES 4

This recipe for breaded chicken breasts proves that sometimes the simplest dishes are the most satisfying. It comes from one of our favorite restaurants in New York, Da Silvano; we like it with a side of spinach sautéed in olive oil and garlic.

1 cup dried bread crumbs
4 boneless chicken breast halves (from two 1-pound breasts)
2 tablespoons olive oil
2 tablespoons unsalted butter
Fine sea salt and freshly ground black pepper
1 lemon, cut into 4 wedges

1 Preheat the oven to 350°F.

2 Spread the bread crumbs on a clean, dry surface and roll the chicken pieces in them to coat all sides, pressing down lightly to make sure the crumbs adhere to the meat.

3 In an ovenproof sauté pan large enough to hold all four breasts, warm the olive oil and melt the butter over medium heat. Add the breaded chicken and cook for 2 minutes on each side, until the bread crumbs are lightly browned. As the chicken cooks, season each side with salt and pepper to taste.

4 Transfer the pan to the oven and bake until the chicken is cooked through, 7 to 10 minutes. Cut one breast open with a knife to check for doneness.

5 Remove the pan from the oven and transfer the breaded chicken to a serving platter. Serve the lemon wedges alongside.

GOOD BEER

It would be hard to miss the Good Beer sign in the window of this basement-level store—each gold letter mimics beer foam dripping over a pint. Every American craft beer is here, organized from East to West Coast in the longest wooden display case one can imagine. The beers all hail from nano- or microbreweries. The ceiling is low, the wood floor is beautiful—all in all, it's the perfect atmosphere for perusing this encyclopedic selection of craft beers. Neither of us has much knowledge of beer, but when we exited the place, we felt we had learned a thing or two about good beer just by browsing the aisles. Take home a few bottles—these hard-to-track-down brews will make you look like a connoisseur, even if all you usually have in your fridge is Budweiser. **3**

HOLYLAND MARKET

Holyland Market is a small treasure at the eastern end of St. Mark's Place. From the outside it is difficult to understand the uniqueness of this market. The exterior of the only Israeli grocery store in Manhattan is blue and covered with graffiti tags, and Israeli newspapers are piled on a metal cart outside. Inside, where Israeli flags hang from the ceiling, the warm and engaging store manager, Eran Hileli, will guide you through the aisles. Hileli opened this kosher store more than a decade ago, but it has the feel of an old-time establishment. All major Israeli and Middle Eastern food brands are offered, and customers come for the tahini, Bamba peanut butter snacks, Elite chocolate bars, pickles, olives, *burekas* (savory phyllo pastries filled with feta cheese, mushrooms, and sometimes spinach), and, of course, the newspapers. **4**

JAPAN PREMIUM BEEF

The best introduction to washugyu beef in New York is found at Japan Premium Beef, a butcher on Great Jones Street. Washugyu is a crossbreed of the famous Japanese black wagyu and the finest American black angus cattle. The washugyu, American Kobe-style beef, is raised in the United States under the supervision of Mr. Yano. It is more cost effective to raise the cattle here than to ship it back to Japan. The breed is 50 percent Tajima waygu/50 percent black angus. They are raised in Oregon, where they are fed dried rice, straw, and grass to help promote the marbling that makes beef tastier. If you want one of the best and probably most expensive beef experiences in New York, visit Japan Premium Beef. Every now and then it is nice to indulge in a great taste treat—this one is definitely worth the expense. **5**

MACARON PARLOUR

Christina Ha learned the craft of making macarons at the famous Ferrandi School in France and, with her husband, Simon Tog, started selling macarons and pastries at the Hester Street Fair on the Lower East Side. When a customer requested an assortment of macarons, it got Christina and Simon thinking about opening a shop. They never looked back! Macaron Parlour is nestled in the heart of the East Village on St. Mark's Place. Making macarons is an art, and you can see Christina at work in the open kitchen, creating them with the flair of a sculptor. The parlour's macarons come in many flavors beyond the traditional vanilla, fig, pistachio, and lemon . . . among them s'mores, red velvet, and candied bacon with maple cream cheese. The Elvis, a peanut butter and caramelized banana macaron, is our favorite. In addition to macarons, the pâtisserie makes cookies and croissants, among other sweet treats. Everything is delicious, but the macarons are divine. **6**

RUSSO'S MOZZARELLA & PASTA

Russo's is a lot more than mozzarella. This tiny Italian grocery, almost hidden behind a giant hand-painted sign, is jammed full of the finest Italian foods. Russo's pasta is made by hand—thick spaghetti, silky thin capellini, hearty manicotti, conchiglie, farfalle, and rotini. Russo's homemade sauces—amatriciana, puttanesca, and marinara—complement aged Parmigiano-Reggiano and Romano cheeses, which can be hand-grated or served in slices with Russo's olives, sausages, and salami. The bread, semolina and white, with or without sesame seeds, is crusty and fresh, ready for dipping into one of the Russo's distinctive extra-virgin olive oils. This tiny shop packs big Italian flavor. **7**

SOS CHEFS

SOS Chefs is a unique New York City treasure: a store that sells thousands of unusual specialty foods. SOS counts more than three hundred professional chefs as customers—and the appeal is obvious. Anyone looking for finger limes from California, pumpkin seeds from Australia, or raisins from the Himalayas; blue grits, orange vinegar, or black lava salt; or fruit and vegetable powders (strawberry juice, spinach, or tomato) can find them here. The floor-to-ceiling apothecary-style cabinets are filled with flavored salts, exotic spices, rice in a rainbow of colors, escargot, argan oil, Iranian pistachios, vanilla beans, black truffles, saffron, and fennel pollen, among many other items that are worth the splurge. Atef Boulaabi and his wife run this amazing shop and source some of the best ingredients in the world. **8**

SUNRISE MART

This Japanese specialty grocery store, one of three in the city, is located on the second floor of a nondescript building. The entrance on the street level is almost unnoticeable. Take the elevator to the second floor and feast your eyes on a cornucopia of Japanese foods and wares. This place is a secret shopping haunt of many New York chefs, as well as students from nearby NYU and Cooper Union who flock here for the myriad fresh and prepared food choices at great prices. Inside the bright space, many roomy aisles offer groceries and snacks, health and beauty items, housewares such as rice cookers and ceramic tableware, and drinks—even the infamous Pokari Sweat, a Japanese version of Gatorade. But the fresh food is the main draw. For a quick, inexpensive lunch, the kitchen's soba noodles, miso soup, and bento boxes are hard to beat. If you don't read Japanese, the friendly staff will happily identify the contents of all those enticing packages, and even give you some idea of what to do with them. The candy and snack section is an eye opener: The packaging is amazing and the Japanese candies have unusually strong but very interesting flavors—some are quite sour; you can even find Kit Kats that come bathed in green tea. You don't have to be Japanese to shop at Sunrise Mart, but you may wish you were after sampling its wares! **9**

10 **10** **10**

TU LU'S BAKERY

In 2009, Tully Lewis and Jen Wells, friends who share a gluten-free lifestyle, opened Tu Lu's bakery in the East Village. Together they have created tasty versions of everything those on a gluten-free diet could wish for, including muffins, brownies, doughnuts, and coffee cakes. Some of their goods are not only gluten-free, but also dairy free, thus suitable for vegans. But you don't have to suffer from gluten sensitivities to enjoy these treats—Tully and Jen have come up with an endless variety of goodies to suit all tastes. Even that all-time favorite red velvet cake is available (either gluten- or dairy-free), along with vanilla, chocolate, and spice cakes, all of which can be frosted with a choice of fifteen different icing flavors. Everything is preservative-free, too, and baked fresh daily on the premises. **10**

ZUCKER BAKERY

With culinary experience at both Daniel and Bouley Bakery under her chef's hat, and inspiration from her family and friends, Zohar Zohar opened Zucker Bakery in 2011. Her creations have Israeli, European, and Moroccan flair and her homemade treats are most special; start with the best-selling sticky buns/cinnamon rolls dubbed Roses. Based on a recipe from Zohar's mother-in-law, which she calls "*shoshanim*," from the Hebrew word for "roses," because of the way the dough is curled into blossom shapes, they are baked daily and sell out very quickly. Other options include Honey Almond Fingers, which are so light and crumbly that you cannot stop at one. Or try the Playdates, a very thin layer of dough spread with a mixture of dates, cinnamon, and cloves, and then rolled. The light, tasty rugelach is Zohar's own version, filled with dates, almonds, and cloves, and her chocolate babka is a masterpiece. Zohar's tried-and-true family recipes will warm your heart and tantalize your taste buds. The place is charming and quiet, so linger awhile over a good cup of coffee and a piece of Love Loaf—a gluten-free cookie featuring a mix of dried fruits and nuts. Our favorite treat is the Alfajores, a dulce de leche–filled sandwich cookie rolled in coconut flakes. **11**

11

11

GREENWICH VILLAGE

Greenwich Village was once a real village, a bucolic escape from the congestion of lower Manhattan. The Village has always been part of American cultural history: Thomas Paine, Henry James, Edith Wharton, James Baldwin, Jack Kerouac, Edward Albee, Lenny Bruce, Janis Joplin, Woody Guthrie, and Woody Allen are just some of the artists who, at one time or another, lived and worked in this intimate part of downtown New York City.

In spite of its celebrities and a few touristy streets, the Village is still a relatively peaceful enclave of large old trees, brick town-houses, small restaurants, and unique shops. Not long ago the food scene was distinctly southern Italian: legendary butcher shops, bak-eries, and grocers. The Village's bohemian coffeehouses started as neighborhood Italian cafés. But with the influx of new ethnic groups and a younger demographic, it has become a truly international and trendy stop on the food trail. In spite of the Village's high celebrity quotient, the food stores here are low-key and friendly with a strong neighborhood feel, very different from what you might expect in a place as famous as Greenwich Village.

AUX MERVEILLEUX DE FRED

Tucked away on a side street at 37 Eighth Avenue is Aux Merveilleux de Fred, a total eye-catcher boasting a huge crystal chandelier that could have decorated a French castle, a stunning marble countertop displaying the delicious Merveilleux pastry, and an open kitchen allowing customers to watch a pastry chef rolling the gems of meringues in various toppings. If you're not familiar with the Merveilleux, you're not alone. This traditional sweet from northern France had fallen out of fashion until the late 1990s, when Fred decided to make it the star of Aux Merveilleux de Fred at his pastry shop in Lille, France. It's a light and airy combination of soft and not-so-soft meringues, held together with flavored whipped cream and rolled in white chocolate flakes, crystallized cherry meringue, or caramelized hazelnuts. It looks a bit like a snowball, and for many, biting into one evokes delicious memories of childhood. They are made in this New York outpost in different sizes, individually in mini, regular, or large sizes, and they come in six different flavors with French names you might find hard to pronounce: *Merveilleux* (chocolate), *Incroyable* (speculoos cream and white chocolate), *Impensable* (coffee), *Excentrique* (cherry), *Magnifique* (praline, almond, hazelnuts), and *Sans-Culotte* (caramel). The shop also sells Cramiques, which are brioche-y breads loaded with raisins or chocolates, or coated with sugar. **1**

CARRY ON TEA & SYMPATHY

Tea & Sympathy was started by Nicky Perry in the early 1990s as a café that sold traditional British fare including shepherd's pies, scones, muffins, sticky pudding, spotted dick, and toad in the hole—all served with tea, of course. Later she bought an adjacent storefront and converted it into a charming grocery with English goodies such as Crunchie bars, Murray Mints, Mars bars, Hobnobs, Maltesers, and more. As soon you enter you feel as if you have been teleported to a village in England. In addition to a variety of teas you will find thick-cut marmalade, Weetabix cereal, mint sauce, Cadbury and Quality Street toffees, puddings . . . and a collection of teapots and teacups with saucers. Lots of pictures of Queen Elizabeth grace not only the walls but the china as well. Nicky and co-owner Sean Kavanagh-Dowsett are there to help with a bit of advice and a wicked sense of English humor. It's all enough to bring tears to the eyes of homesick expats. **2**

FAICCO'S PORK STORE

Bleecker Street was once lined with pushcarts selling fruits, vegetables, breads, and other basics for the home cupboard. When Joseph Faicco opened this store in 1950, he couldn't afford refrigeration so he restocked the sausage every morning, and in the process earned a reputation for making the freshest pork sausage on the block. Faicco's habit of making sausage daily continues to the present. Early each morning the kitchen crew grinds pork, adds seasonings, and stuffs that day's supply of sausages. The truth is that Faicco has to make sausage fresh every day because, by day's end, it's sold out. You can choose hot or sweet, with or without garlic, cheese, fennel, or parsley. Try the sweet fennel-flavored pork sausage, excellent in marinara over penne pasta. At lunchtime neighborhood regulars line up for their submarine-sized sandwiches. This is a neighborhood treasure not to be missed.**3**

FAICCO'S TENDER PORK CUTLETS

Faicco's Pork Store

SERVES 4

This recipe lets the quality of Faicco's pork shine through—with just enough flavoring to add interest, but not enough to mask the delicate, fresh taste of the succulent cutlets.

2 large eggs
3 tablespoons whole milk
½ teaspoon salt
Pinch of freshly ground black pepper
1 cup bread crumbs
1½ pounds boneless pork cutlets, preferably from Faicco's
½ cup extra-virgin olive oil
2 tablespoons chopped fresh parsley

1 Beat the eggs and milk in a bowl. In a separate bowl, combine the salt, pepper, and bread crumbs.

2 One at a time, dip the pork cutlets in the egg mixture and the bread crumbs and place on a plate.

3 When all the cutlets are coated, heat the oil in a large frying pan over medium heat until a pinch of bread crumbs dropped into the oil sizzles immediately. Add the cutlets to the pan and cook for about 5 minutes per side, until lightly browned.

4 Drain the cutlets on paper towels. Serve hot, garnished with the parsley.

FLORENCE PRIME MEAT MARKET

Florence is the butcher shop that many New Yorkers consider their own personal secret. How many times have we been collared by someone who told us, "There's a tiny butcher shop off the map in the Village that sells aged prime meat at insanely low prices"? Florence is amazing, but it is no longer a secret: Most Villagers know that Florence is a contender for the best butcher in the city.

The beef here is prime Angus, dry-aged on the premises for more than three weeks. One of the specialties is Newport Steak, a strip steak cut from the sirloin, less chewy than rump steak and less fatty than a short loin strip. Florence has an old-time feel, with sawdust on the floor and a meat locker with a big wooden door. The owner, Benny Pizzuco, is a master butcher, as ample as his shop, and his helpers couldn't be friendlier. When we met Pizzuco he was working behind the counter on another specialty—veal shoulder, great for blanquette de veau, braised veal shoulder, or a simple veal stew. **4**

JACQUES TORRES

The charismatic Jacques Torres combines an impeccable sense of style with total mastery of the art of making chocolate. Known as Mr. Chocolate, Torres grew up in France and was originally trained as a pastry chef, but his passion for chocolate led him to become an artisan chocolatier, making his own chocolates, starting with the cacao beans and designing the finished products.

The Jacques Torres corner store on Hudson Street (not to mention his seven other locations) is not your ordinary chocolate shop. The chocolates are handcrafted using the purest, all-natural ingredients available. Although the chocolate shapes are traditional, the tastes are superior and unusual: Fresh Squeezed Lemon and Raspberry Lemon are among our favorites. There is a large selection, starting with truffles and continuing on to bars, barks, and assorted chocolates in boxes. It seems that Torres will cover anything with chocolate including marshmallows, raisins, nuts, espresso beans, Cheerios, and even potato chips. This is a great place to enjoy a hot chocolate, accompanied by one of Torres's famous chocolate chip cookies, which are gooey inside and crisp around the edges. **5**

6

MAGNOLIA BAKERY

There are visionaries even in the world of cupcakes. Alyssa Torey, founder of Magnolia Bakery, is the Isaac Newton of her world. When Torey opened Magnolia Bakery in 1996, no one had a clue that cupcake love would sweep the country, but Torey converted a rundown Bleecker Street store into a pastel fantasy, and now, despite many attempts to replicate her concept, lines of cupcake lovers still stretch around the block waiting patiently for her pink, blue, yellow, and pastel wonders. The anatomy of the cupcake is simple: white, chocolate, or red velvet cake covered in buttery pastel-colored frostings. The simplest foods are frequently the hardest to make well, and Magnolia's attention to quality ingredients and fine detail makes these cupcakes some of the best we've tried. Magnolia is not just about cupcakes; the thick-frosted full-sized layer cakes are a real American comfort food. Don't miss the banana pudding, the Snickers icebox pie, and the caramel mini cheesecake. Everything is baked from scratch in the store's ovens, then iced by hand before your eyes. Torey has moved on to other ventures, but Magnolia remains tried and true. **6**

THE MEADOW

The Meadow opened in Portland, Oregon, in 2006 and came to the West Village in 2010. The very small but seductive shop is one of our favorite stores in town. The window is filled with salt blocks in every shape and size, catching light from the outdoors—you can't help but walk in. Although salt is an ancient ingredient that has the power to enhance the flavor of an assortment of foods, for the longest time, it was used only for savory foods. Today salt is incorporated into sweet foods ranging from chocolate and cake to cookies, ice cream, and fruit desserts, making this shop irresistible to anyone who likes to cook or bake. The Meadow specializes in artisan salt from around the world in many textures and a range of colors from black to pink to gray and, of course, white. The offerings include more than 110 sea salts and quarried salts from over twenty-six countries. The shop also sells three hundred varieties of chocolate from some of the best chocolate makers around the world. The selection of bitters is so extensive that it draws mixologists from all over the city. The center of the store features a large table filled with beautiful fragrant flowers. Between the salt, chocolate, bitters, and flowers this shop is an essential destination not only for New Yorkers but for anyone who visits from anywhere in the world. **7**

MURRAY'S CHEESE

Murray's Cheese opened in 1940 as an egg and cheese shop catering to the Italian community on and around Bleecker Street. It's the oldest cheese shop in New York City, and many consider it to be the best as well. The *New York Times* has hailed Murray's as a "local landmark" and "a mecca for New Yorkers" while Forbes.com declared it the "world's best cheese shop." After Rob Kaufelt, the current owner, bought Murray's in the early nineties, he scoured the world for the most unusual artisan cheeses being produced, from California to Vermont, Wales to Athens, and just about everywhere in between. Through his passion, love, and knowledge of cheese and the food business, Kaufelt has not only managed to double the size of the store, he has created a cheese emporium like no other.

Back in the 1940s, when Murray's first opened, for most Americans, cheese came in two colors—white and yellow—and one shape: square. Cheese that was ooey, gooey, and smelly was not yet de rigueur at cocktail parties. Real cheese was considered a fancy food for people who spoke French. A true believer in the power of cheese, Kaufelt fought back against this deep cultural resistance when he took over the store. He believed that he could convert the masses by getting them to taste cheese the way it was meant to be tasted. New Yorkers discovered Murray's, and thus began their love affair with cheese.

The first thing you'll notice in Murray's sparkling shop is the row of cheese refrigerators. There you'll find over 250 varieties of goat, sheep, cow, and buffalo milk cheeses, along with sausage, saucisson, ham, and prosciutto. One of the secrets behind Murray's is the basement cheese cave, where cheese is stored at precisely the right temperature and humidity to ensure that it is aged properly. If you find the massive selection daunting, the managers will be more than happy to cut you a few samples along the way. **8**

GALA PORK PIE
Pork meat, a delicate blend of herbs and spices with boiled egg center.
$7.95   ½ $4.00

MyersofKeswick.com

634

mixed berries
popSorbetto

pumpkin pie
popGelato

MARMITE
YEAST EXTRACT

9
9
9
9
9
11
11

MYERS OF KESWICK

Myers of Keswick, a small shop on Hudson Street not far from the White Horse Tavern, is a perfect replica of an English grocer, circa 1935. Keswick is a small Cornwall village, and the store bills itself as "That Bastard of Albion in Manhattan." You enter the shop through a wooden screen door on squeaky springs. The decor is so convincing that you would be only mildly surprised if Jeeves came by looking for a can of Morton's Mushy Peas or a packet of loose tea from Taylor's at Harrowgate. Keswick's keen sense of kitsch goes straight to the Queen Elizabeth dishtowels.

On one side, you'll see neat stacks of English canned and packaged foods, mostly beans and teas. On the other side, on the white-enameled butcher counter, you will find pies and sausages—pork pies, sausage rolls, and Cornish pasties made in house and sold under the shop's English Glory label. The steak and kidney pie is good enough to convince at least one Frenchwoman that English cooking does, in fact, have some merit. Stop in, pick up some bangers and kidney pie, and discover that you don't have to be born in the U.K. to appreciate English food. **9**

OTTOMANELLI & SONS

Although many stores around New York City carry the Ottomanelli name, this butcher shop is the true original. The Ottomanelli family has occupied this address for more than sixty years; the decor is unchanged, the same butchers are here year after year, and the quality is just as consistent. Ottomanelli's is famous citywide, if only for its unrivaled selection of wild game. This is the source for a few pounds of alligator or rattlesnake meat, both sold fresh. You will also find ostrich steaks, kangaroo, venison, buffalo, antelope, and wild turkey. For those in a more traditional mood, the chicken and beef are excellent. But the next time you crave exotic meat, call Frank, a son of the founder, and he'll have it ready and waiting. **10**

POPBAR

Popbar is one of the most popular spots on Carmine Street. The gelato, sorbet, and yogurt pops served by the cheerful team in this fun atmosphere will turn you into a popaholic on your first visit. All the ingredients are pure, with no artificial flavors, colors, or preservatives; only fresh fruits are used. The popGelato (gelato on a stick) is handmade daily in special molds designed by the company. The flavors are seasonal and many can be dipped in dark chocolate, white chocolate, nuts, or sprinkles. The YogurtPop, made with fresh fruit, comes in classic, strawberry flavored, and chocolate-dipped versions. The popBites—small gelato or sorbet treats coated with chocolate and sprinkles—will brighten all your parties. In the winter, if you prefer something warm, try their hot chocolate on a stick: Just dip it into steamed milk to create your own dark, milk, or white chocolaty goodness. **11**

IRISH COFFEE
Porto Rico Importing Company

SERVES 1

This excellent coffee cocktail, delicious with or without whipped cream, can be a template for endless variations. Omitting the alcohol works, too.

- 1½ ounces Irish whiskey, at room temperature
- 2 tablespoons brown sugar
- 6 ounces hot coffee, preferably from Porto Rico Importing Company
- 2 tablespoons whipped cream
- Dash of ground nutmeg

1 Warm up your mug under hot running water for a few minutes, then dry it.

2 Add the whiskey, brown sugar, and coffee to the mug and stir until the sugar dissolves. Top with the whipped cream and the nutmeg. Serve immediately.

PORTO RICO IMPORTING COMPANY

It's a delight to discover Porto Rico Importing Company, purveyor and roaster of coffee beans since 1907. Before you even step inside you smell the coffee. Porto Rico offers unblended coffees from South and Central America, Africa, the Caribbean, India, Indonesia, and the Pacific. Multicolored burlap sacks of coffee and tins of tea line the floor and walls. Choose from twenty-two French roasts and twenty-six decaffeinated varieties, to name just two categories. The nearly infinite varieties of blends can be confusing; as a start, we were intrigued by Swiss Chocolate, French Vanilla Bean, Tiramisù, DeCaf Strudel, and Double Nut Fudge. Porto Rico coffee is mixed in Williamsburg and brought to the store, fresh from the roaster. After you peruse the coffee selection you can concentrate on the teas; these include blends such as chai ginseng, licorice, spice herbal, tea sachets in boxes, and house blends, including Russian caravan and Ceylon mint, along with white, black, green, oolong, decaffeinated, rooibos, herbal blends . . . and more. There is no place to sit in this tiny coffee haven—you won't find anybody hunched over a laptop. What you will find are great coffee blends to take home and savor. **12**

SOCKERBIT

Sockerbit, which means "sugar cube" in Swedish, is a white, minimalist store full of just that, and so much more: jellies, gummies, chewy things, crunchy things, gooey things, rolled things, and mushy things—lots of yummy things that stick to your teeth, in just about every shape, size, color, and flavor you can imagine. The candies, which are housed in clear drawers that line an entire wall of this bright and extraordinarily alluring shop on Christopher Street, are accompanied by descriptive labels, so even though the sweets are Swedish, you don't have to guess what you are about to enjoy. The idea is that you compose your own bag of candy out of more than one hundred choices (all of which are made with natural ingredients and food colors derived from nature). The owners, Swedish-born Stefan Ernberg and his Argentinian wife, Florencia Baras, have succeeded in creating an inviting space where *smågodis*, ("little candies") are the star attraction. **13**

SULLIVAN STREET TEA & SPICE COMPANY

Once the headquarters of the Triangle Social Club, an infamous Mafia hangout run by Genovese crime-family boss Vincent "the Chin" Gigante, this Old World space is now home to an impressive selection of teas, herbs, and spices from around the globe. Times have changed since its days as a Mafia meeting place, but proprietor Mark Greenberg has preserved the original mosaic-tile floors, tin ceiling, and antique mural. In addition to organic teas and more than 150 spices, this charming store sells kitchen gadgets—from spice grinders to nutmeg shavers—and Himalayan salt in blocks, crystals, or powder, which can be used for cooking or in a hot, relaxing bath. Tea is served most of the day, and the friendly staff will answer any question you have about their products. **14**

HARLEM

When people think of Harlem, they think of jazz, churches, great food, and Dapper Dan's boutique. Though many years have passed since the Harlem Renaissance of the 1920s, these hallmarks of old Harlem can still be found today amid new artisan bakeries, coffee shops, and restaurants. Originally settled as a suburb of New York City, Harlem was home to many Dutch immigrants. From 1915 through the 1970s, the neighborhood demographics were drastically altered as African American families migrated from the South and made Harlem their home. Known for its music legends, the Apollo Theater, and literary giants such as Langston Hughes, Harlem's cultural influence on New York City and beyond is legendary. Now in its second renaissance, this neighborhood has revitalized its culinary reputation. Beginning in the early 1990s, President Bill Clinton, who established his foundation and office space there in 2001, was instrumental in the gentrification movement. In a speech in 2001, he observed, "Harlem always struck me as a place that was human and alive, where there was a rhythm to life and a song in the heart, where no matter how bad it was, people held up their heads and went on, and where, when things got good, people were grateful and cared about their neighbors." The real estate boom is ever present here and the food industry has followed suit. A few of our favorite restaurants are Red Rooster, the Cecil, and, of course, Sylvia's. An evening at any one of these establishments is memorable, as are the diverse neighborhood food shops.

EL TEPEYAC GROCERY

If you need to practice your cross-country skiing in the winter and your skateboarding the rest of the year, this is the store for you. High on a hill on Lexington Avenue is the East Harlem grocer El Tepeyac. A plastic palm tree sits at the front door, inviting you into a tiny Mexican food emporium that caters to the Latino population and anyone else who wants to make an authentic Mexican meal. Along with pan dulce, Mexican snacks and drinks, queso fresco, and specialty fruits and vegetables, you can buy the dishes and decor to make your meal completely authentic. The shelves are piled high with Mexican pottery, religious statues, and candles. This charming store is a little bit of Mexico in East Harlem. **1**

FAIRWAY

Fairway is a megamarket con brio. Each of these vast stores is wired into New York's human energy grid, humming and crackling with activity. Shopping at Fairway is like being at a town meeting with complete strangers discussing the quality of the grapefruit or the bargains in the cheese department. The swarms of shoppers circulate around vibrant hills of fruits and vegetables, pyramids of olive oil cans, and architectural follies made of chocolate bars. And everyone jokes that you need an anorak to enter the frozen department. Fairway is committed to promoting small worldwide brands, which you can identify thanks to the labels on the displays that explain the origin of each one.

In addition to the fantastic produce, fresh bread, health food, butcher, and gigantic fish department there is a vast selection of cheese, and staff on hand to explain each one. The olives come in every size and color, and you can buy anything pickled that you can think of. Fairway is committed to delivering the highest-quality foods at the best prices in the city. Take a trip to the Harlem store and be prepared to linger. There is ample parking and it is convenient to public transportation. This is a food adventure you will not soon forget. **2**

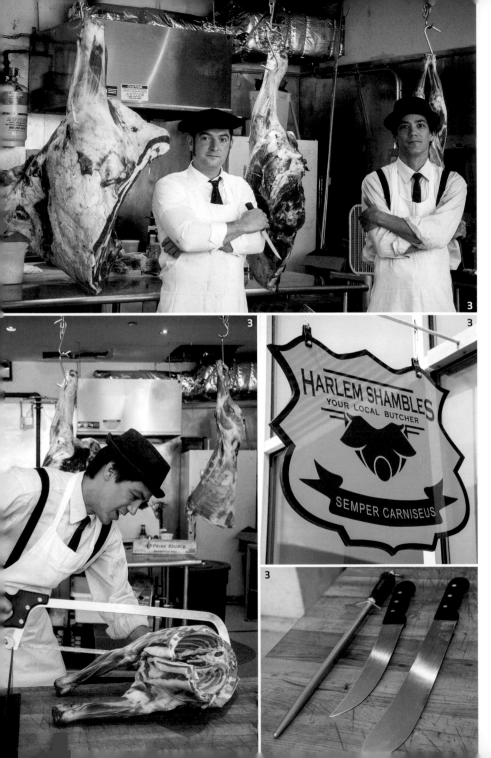

HARLEM SHAMBLES

Harlem has gone green! As you walk around the neighborhood, you'll spot tiny vegetable gardens, fresh eggs for sale laid by chickens living in local community gardens, and the one and only local butcher specializing in grass-fed, antibiotic- and hormone-free meat. Harlem Shambles, owned by Tim and Mark Forrester, resembles the neighborhood butcher you would expect to find in a bucolic European village, including the beret atop Mark's head and the suspenders holding up the brothers' trousers. A few times a week, the pair receive meat from upstate farmers and, with the adeptness of surgeons, use their sharp knives to artfully cut open the carcasses, remove the fat, debone the legs, separate the belly from the loin… and so on. They are indeed culinary sculptors. The meat is well priced, and the quality is equal to some of the fanciest butchers in the city. In addition to the classic cuts, it is also one of the few butcher shops where you can find a large variety of unusual goodies. Stop by for their homemade sausages, including chorizo, merguez, and hot and sweet Italian options, and for fresh eggs from the same farmers who supply their meat. **3**

LEVAIN BAKERY

Levain Bakery's second location (the original is on the Upper West Side) is a tiny shop that typically entices a line of neighborhood regulars but also customers from all over the world who have heard about the legendary baked goods, especially the shop's famous six-ounce chocolate chip walnut cookie. The bakery was founded in 1994 by friends Connie McDonald and Pam Weekes. McDonald was in banking and Weekes was in fashion; both were competitive swimmers and training for the Ironman. The workouts left them hungry for something tasty to eat, and thus a great chocolate chip cookie was created. Following that masterstroke, the duo devised their oatmeal raisin cookie, dark chocolate chip cookie, and dark chocolate peanut butter cookie. The cookies are extraordinary right out of the oven, but take some home and grab a glass of milk, and you will have a preview of heaven. Cookies aside, the blueberry muffin is almost all top and the chocolate chip brioche is a chocolate lover's prize. We can never decide between the bomboloncini (small jelly doughnut) and the sticky bun, so we just buy both and indulge. **4**

MAKE MY CAKE

Make My Cake opened decades ago, and the delicious offerings at this bakery are based on family recipes that incorporate the culinary heritage of the South—from Mississippi to Alabama—and what the bakery refers to as "Harlem soul." Ma Smith, as she was affectionately called, was the matriarch of the family business. She handed down her cake, pie, and cookie recipes to daughter Jo-Ann and granddaughter Aliyah. Several generations later, these keepers of the family recipes continue to uphold the legacy of "good taste" that runs in the family. The popularity of these baked goods is contagious: Make My Cake is a beloved destination for thousands of visitors from around the world seeking the ultimate red velvet cake and various other heavenly desserts. Other sweet creations that have put the bakery on the map include German chocolate cake, carrot cake, and sweet potato cheesecake, a local favorite. Both locations in Harlem are warm and inviting and are certain to satisfy your sweet tooth. **5**

4

4

4

5

LITTLE ITALY

The Little Italy of great restaurants, passionate people, and tough customers is a neighborhood in transition. Though many of the original immigrant families have relocated to the outer boroughs and suburbs, you can still see old men on their folding chairs in front of tenement buildings while, above them, old women lean on window-sills, pillows beneath their arms. But these days they're not watching kids playing stickball in the street; they're watching an endless stream of the young, the trendy, and the beautiful.

While walking Mott and Mulberry Streets, you can hear tour guides call out the holy sites of pop culture: "This is where *The Godfather* was filmed. This is where Joey Gallo was shot." You can even take *The Sopranos* tour. Many of the original businesses are gone or have been theme-parked beyond all recognition, but the neighborhood still maintains its scaled-down charm. At one time, Little Italy was home to thousands of immigrants from southern Italy, and the food stores and restaurants still evoke that distinctive Neapolitan or Sicilian flavor. To add to that flavor, every September 19 a statue of Saint Gennaro, the principal patron saint of Naples, is taken from its permanent place in the Church of the Most Precious Blood on Mulberry Street and carried in joyous procession through the streets of Little Italy. The weeklong Festival of San Gennaro is not to be missed. Booths offering everything from sausages and onions to "Kiss Me I'm Italian" T-shirts line the gaudily lit streets. For a brief time every year these few blocks of downtown Manhattan look and feel like Naples. But whenever you go to Little Italy, look closely and you will find wonderful food stores with authentic character and quality.

ALLEVA DAIRY

Alleva is one of Little Italy's last remaining mozzarella makers. The store, run by the fourth and fifth generations of the Alleva family, has been in business for more than a century. In Italy there's a *latteria* in just about every village, but handmade mozzarella is becoming harder to find in New York, and the difference between the stuff made by hand and by machine is like Camembert and Velveeta. Alleva makes mozzarella fresh every morning and delivers the cheese to restaurants all over the city. The day begins with curds, made fresh from whole or skim milk. The curds are mixed with fresh milk in a large steaming jar, then shaped by hand into a white ball before being set to cure in a vat of cold water, salted or unsalted. Alleva still displays its antique gilded glass signs advertising "Burro e uova" ("butter and eggs") and "Latticini di Nostra Produzione" ("mozzarella and fresh ricotta made here.")[1]

BLACK SEED BAGELS

To begin this tasty journey, there's Stumptown Coffee, then there's the shop's mantra, which, according to co-owner Noah Bernamoff, is nothing less than "to capture the best of Montreal and New York bagels, basically a little sweet, a little salty; dense and chewy, but equally light and airy; heavily seeded but firm and just a little waxy." Although the phrase "powerful sesame seed" certainly may seem like an oxymoron, this tiny black or white seed offers so much more than a distinct nutty flavor. It is a powerhouse of organic minerals, especially calcium, and is an alkaline food that supports bone and general health. That's exactly why sesame seeds made it to the shop's list of "foundation foods." And, at Black Seed, the bagels are generously coated in seeds, making them a healthy treat. These are such perfect examples of bagels, you'll want to eat several of them. They come in all the classic flavors, including everything, salt, and poppy seed, and you can choose from house-made spreads that run the gamut from lox and dill to almond butter. We were fortunate enough to go into the kitchen to see chef Dianna Daoheung deftly taking the dough in her small hands and quickly turning it one by one into artfully shaped bagels. The raw dough is quickly immersed in hot water and then placed on wood planks, where it's covered in black or white sesame seeds, onions, salt, or everything. These are New York bagels at their best. **2**

CECI-CELA PATISSERIE

Nestled in a petite shop on Spring Street, Ceci-Cela is a French patisserie par excellence founded by Chef Laurent Dupal, who has presided over its offerings for more than fifteen years. The sign here reads "patisserie des connaisseurs," and though her team of pastry chefs may not know how to spell connoisseurs, they do know how to bake for them. The pastry case in this long, narrow store is filled with the croissants, tartes sucrées, financiers, tart aux raisins, and mille-feuilles that, year after year, put Ceci-Cela at the top of nearly every pastry poll in New York City. You might have to wait in line for their famous chocolate éclairs but the wait is well worth it. A Parisian bus stop sign stands at the entrance of Ceci-Cela, so you can dream of Paris while you are on line. **3**

DESPAÑA AND DESPAÑA VINOS Y MÁS

There are plenty of bodegas in Manhattan, but only Despaña sells food products exclusively from Spain. Despaña started in Queens in 1971 as a chorizo factory. Despaña in Little Italy is done up like a trendy Madrid tapaseria—wood floors, marble counters, long black shelves filled with Spanish groceries, an open kitchen, and a café in the back that is not to be missed. Starting in the morning and all day long, samples of cheese, chorizo, and olives are arranged on the tasting counter. Here you can pick up one of Despaña's homemade chorizos: chorizo picante, chorizo de cantimpalo, and chorizo chistorra, all prepared with the famous spice, Pimentón de la Vera,

which provides the unique flavor and color of the chorizo. If you like prosciutto, check out the many Spanish varieties displayed in the window, including pata negra and iberico, which you can buy by the slice or in bulk. (Each whole ham weighs about fifteen pounds, but for your convenience the store offers classes in the art of slicing.) Despaña is so inviting you'll want to stay awhile and peruse the shelves of olive oils, vinegars, jars of vegetables, fruit preserves, sardines, anchovies, rice for risotto, fifty different kinds of cheeses, and, of course, an array of excellent bocadillo (Spanish sandwiches) and other prepared foods. Don't forget to stop by the wine store next door. Despaña Vinos y Más offers a selection of wines and spirits from Spain—plus wine tastings every week. The only thing missing from Despaña is Spanish lessons. **4**

SALMOREJO
(CHILLED TOMATO SOUP)
Despaña

SERVES 4 TO 6

Thanks to Inma Barrero, a great ceramic artist and wonderful cook, for this delicious recipe from Córdoba, Spain.

2¼ pounds mature red tomatoes
2 cloves garlic
1 tablespoon salt
2 tablespoons red wine vinegar
2¼ cups dry white bread crumbs
⅔ cup extra-virgin olive oil

FOR THE GARNISH
4 hard-boiled eggs, peeled and cut into small pieces
3½ ounces jamón serrano, cut into small dice

1 In a blender, puree the tomatoes with the garlic and salt, then add the vinegar and the bread crumbs and blend until combined. With the blender still running, slowly add the olive oil.

2 Pour the soup into a bowl and refrigerate until well chilled. Just before serving, toss together the eggs and ham. Serve the soup cold, garnished with the eggs and ham.

DI PALO'S FINE FOODS

On Broome Street, you can now find Italian grocery stores that sell sushi. At Di Palo's salumeria you won't find a trace of toro. What you will see in this newly renovated store are huge stacked wheels of Parmigiano-Reggiano and giant hanging bulbs of Asiago gently aging in the natural light of the store windows. Inside you will find an enormous selection of Italian cheeses, olive oil, vinegar, and packaged foods. Be prepared to wait: Customers take numbers from a machine, and it's not unusual to find yourself twenty numbers down the list. At Di Palo's the wait is so long because the food is so good and the service so attentive. The counterman will insist that you try several kinds of cheese or olive oil before you make your choice. Lou Di Palo, whose great-grandfather founded the store, scours the Italian countryside for anything new that strikes his eye and his palate—olive oils from obscure farms and a selection of balsamic vinegars, including one aged for over one hundred years. Lou knows every producer by name and can tell you the exact quality of the air, soil, and water that gave birth to your olives, pimientos, or canned tomatoes. He will also tell you about St. Eustachio coffee, slowly roasted on wood for sweetness. If you are here on a Friday or Saturday, stand in line for the creamy burrata mozzarella just flown in from Rome and sold out within hours of its arrival. Di Palo and his family work hard to keep things Italian in Little Italy. **5**

ENOTECA DI PALO

In 2010, the new generation of Di Palos opened a wine store selling Italian wines. It is strategically located next to the family's legendary store, Di Palo's Fine Foods. You can pick up some crusty Italian bread, some artisanal Italian cheese and salumi, and walk right next door for a bottle of terrific Italian wine. Sam Di Palo visited some of the best wineries in Italy and brought back the best of the smaller producers to Grand Street. A great Italian food and wine experience awaits. **6**

PAPABUBBLE

This unpretentious little candy store is easy to miss, but to do so would be tragic. The owners, Fiona Ryan and Chris Grassi, hold multiple candy workshops every day, so Papabubble's customers can watch the entire process, from cooking to coloring, flavoring, shaping, and eating! Sure you can enter the store, make a purchase, and leave, but you miss out if you do not wait for the performance, which occurs every few hours and takes about one and a half hours. Opened in 2007, the store is part laboratory, part kitchen, with glass shelves containing rows of flasks, containers, and utensils. Opposite the kitchen are inviting jars of eye-catching handmade candy. There are lollipops and candies in flavors like cinnamon, strawberry, licorice, mint, anise, and lime, all in amusing shapes like bears, rings, toothbrushes, knots, tigers, glasses, bunnies—and even dentures. **7**

PIEMONTE RAVIOLI

Security at Piemonte Ravioli is tight: only family members are allowed access to the kitchen. They have guarded their secret pasta recipe since 1920, and such vigilance is justified. The store's brochure, printed daily, lists forty-eight different varieties of pasta—fresh, dry, and frozen—and three sizes of ravioli in multiple flavors, including pumpkin, sun-dried tomato, and Gorgonzola. Piemonte also sells homemade sauces: Bolognese, pesto, puttanesca, and amatriciana. Many stores in Little Italy have undergone cosmetic surgery, but this little store has aged gracefully. Nothing fancy here, just good store-made tortellini, cannelloni, and stuffed shells along with specialty Italian groceries. **8**

WINE THERAPY

Neighborhood residents exclaim, "I love my wine store!" Wine Therapy is a small, charming store with hand-selected boutique wines at great prices. The owner, a Frenchman named Jean-Baptiste Humbert, who opened the shop in 2005, specializes in organic, biodynamic wines from around the world. These wines are made using natural yeast and low levels of sulfites, and are devoid of chemical intervention throughout the winemaking process. Luckily for Humbert, and the rest of us, his father lives in France and helps source wines from smaller-scale producers who treat their land with love. **9**

LOWER EAST SIDE

Across Houston Street from the East Village is the Lower East Side. This neighborhood is, for many Americans, a Jewish homeland second only to Israel. At the turn of the nineteenth century, a new wave of Jewish immigrants from central Europe came ashore, where the garment industry was born, where some of New York's oldest synagogues still stand, and where you will still find New York's most famous Jewish food stores: pickle vendors, pastrami makers, bakers, and delicatessens. Third- and fourth-generation Jewish families continue to come into Manhattan from suburbia to show their kids the wonders of Katz's Deli, where during World War II the battle cry was "Send a salami to your boy in the army." In the 1950s and '60s, the Lower East Side absorbed waves of immigration from Puerto Rico and the Dominican Republic. And, more recently, a new generation of food pioneers has moved into the neighborhood, opening edgy stores that add new flavor to the already rich culinary landscape. The Lower East Side still boasts the flavor of years past but it's also become a hot spot for the young and trendy.

BISOUS CIAO

The Lower East Side is best known for its Jewish shops, such as Gertel's Bakery (now closed), Kossar's Bialys, and Economy Candy, rather than stores selling small French delicacies such as the macaron, that crunchy meringue-based sandwich cookie that has become all the rage in recent years. Bisous Ciao, which specializes in these brightly colored confections, is located on Stanton Street, a mile-long stretch that retains its old-time neighborhood feeling.

Owner Tanya Ngangan runs back and forth between the kitchen, in the back of the shop, and the front of the store to help customers choose from one of the many flavors, some of which are unique to the shop. We loved the macarons inspired by Ngangan's mother, who owns a Thai restaurant: white chocolate ganache infused with Thai tea leaves, black sesame, green tea and masala chai, and yuzu. There are the standard flavors, such as bitter chocolate and vanilla hazelnut, but these change seasonally. Bisous Ciao macarons are available individually or in boxes. If you cannot visit Ngangan's adorable shop on the Lower East Side (or her second shop in the West Village), her macarons are available online. You can even custom-design a saying such as "Keep Calm and Eat a Macaron," and voilà, it will be airbrushed onto your macarons. It's guaranteed: Eating these delectable creations will calm you. **1**

DOUGHNUT PLANT

Mark Israel began his doughnut empire with a family recipe he found by chance among his grandfather's papers. With no money to rent space, he began making small batches in the basement of his Lower East Side tenement. He delivered his doughnuts by bicycle to a few sympathetic local coffee shops. But these were no ordinary crullers; these were the masterworks of a doughnut virtuoso. Before long, orders overwhelmed capacity, and in 1994 Israel started the Doughnut Plant on Grand Street; the word was out and lines formed quickly. At the Doughnut Plant, things start cooking just as the most devoted night birds are heading home. The expert team of bakers mixes batches of all-natural batter, then hand-cuts the dough into doughnut shapes. Set aside to rise for an hour, the doughnuts then go for a short dip in the fryer. Israel uses chopsticks to turn the doughnuts in the fryer, then carefully places each one on a wire rack. Israel is a big guy with a big heart, and his doughnuts are a labor of love—he repeats this process for forty different flavors, or about two thousand doughnuts, at the Grand Street location every day. He's also added a few other locations—and the doughnuts (along with coffee) are available for delivery to Manhattan, Brooklyn, and Queens. **2**

ECONOMY CANDY

Economy Candy is now a third-generation emporium for serious sweet tooths, managed by Jerry Cohen, his wife, Liene, and his son Mitchell. Members of the Cohen family have been running Economy Candy since 1937, and it's still going strong for anyone needing a sugar fix. The jam-packed store sells just about every type of commercial candy imaginable, in every size, shape, and color. If you have fond memories of candy buttons stuck on white paper strips, Sugar Daddies, nonpareils, Bonomo's Turkish Taffy, Baby Ruth bars, Red Hots, Clark Bars, and Almond Joys, they are all up for grabs, plus much more. The shelves are precariously balanced, tons of candy on the verge of tumbling down at any moment. You can buy a quarter pound (or fifty pounds) of your favorite candy and have it shipped anywhere in the world if you like. At Economy Candy, with its vast selection of treats from everyone's childhood, even an amnesiac would wax nostalgic. **3**

ESSEX STREET MARKET

We like the authentic feel of Essex Street Market, which was started by Mayor Fiorello La Guardia in the 1940s to give pushcarts an indoor home. At that time the market served the neighborhood's predominantly Jewish and Italian populations. This changed in the 1950s with the influx of Puerto Rican immigrants and continues to evolve with the hipsters who are coming in droves to this trendy neighborhood. This market reflects the history of immigration and change in one of the greatest cities in the United States.

Many of the vendors have been here for years. Luis Batista opened his shop more than twenty years ago. This Hispanic grocery, along with Viva Fruits & Vegetables, specializes in Latin American foods. Both places offer an excellent selection of exotic fruits such as plantains, sugarcane, cassava, coconuts, and papaya. The grocery items include things like tortillas, tacos, and hard-to-find spices, and you can get recommendations for just about anything Latin. In addition to the stores described here, there is a butcher, an ice-cream maker, and a chocolatier, as well as fishmongers and cheese stores, such as Saxelby, which is at the entrance and carries an impressive array of American cheeses and yogurts. Begin here for a satisfying food journey. 4

Ni Japanese Delicacies

Atsushi Numata, the owner of Ni Japanese Delicacies, hides behind the counter in his tiny kitchen making some of the best Japanese bites for takeout. The counter is piled so high with Japanese groceries it is hard to tell how all the fresh food appears, but you make your choice and Atsushi deftly creates your dish at lightning speed. And, as they say in Japanese, it is all *oishi* (delicious)!

Pain d'Avignon

At Pain d'Avignon you can buy this bakery's version of pain aux raisins, which they call "escargots" because of their snail-like shape. The escargots come in almond and pistachio-chocolate flavors. All the breads and pastries are delicious, but Pain d'Avignon has loyal followers for their baguettes, and cranberry-pecan and seven-grain breads. Many food critics consider it one of the best bakeries in the city. Enjoy a big taste of Paris in this tiny shop.

Peasant Stock

Owned by Christine Juritsch, Peasant Stock specializes in a roster of flavorful soups that changes daily, plus cornbread and Irish soda bread on the side. Christine's husband helped her decorate this little shop with a tiny stove that produces some knock-your-socks-off soup flavors such as organic French lentil, peas and leeks, and lemon chicken chorizo. She told us, "I have created a perfect job for myself," and day after day, her faithful customers return to prove it.

GIGOT DE SEPT HEURES (SEVEN-HOUR LEG OF LAMB)
Essex Street Market

SERVES 6

For a glorious Sunday lunch (typically followed by a nap), French mothers used to make this recipe for leg of lamb for their families. The cooking was often started the night before, and throughout the morning the household was tantalized by the aroma of the slow-cooking meat. *Gigot de sept heures* is also one of the oldest traditional Easter recipes. The leftovers make a great pasta sauce the next day.

5- to 6-pound leg of lamb, with bone
½ cup olive oil
½ cup rum
5 large carrots, cut into large chunks
1 stalk celery, finely chopped
1 bulb fennel, finely chopped
20 shallots, peeled and left whole
5 strips orange zest
½ cup sugar
Salt and freshly ground pepper

1 In a large casserole or Dutch oven, bring water to a boil over high heat, then carefully add the leg of lamb, making sure it's completely covered with water, and boil for 5 minutes; remove from the water and pat dry. Discard the cooking water and dry the casserole.

2 Heat the oil in the casserole over high heat, add the leg of lamb, and brown it on all sides.

3 Pour the rum over the lamb and use a long match or a lighter to carefully ignite the rum.

4 Reduce the heat to low and add the carrots, celery, fennel, shallots, and orange zest. Cover the pot and cook for 6 hours, turning the lamb every hour.

5 Uncover the casserole, stir in the sugar, and cook, uncovered, over very low heat for 1 hour more. Carefully transfer the meat and vegetables to a platter. If the sauce is too thin, cook over high heat until it has reduced and thickened. Season with salt and pepper and serve immediately.

KATZ'S DELICATESSEN

A table in the middle of the restaurant displays a sign, *When Harry Met Sally*—recalling the famous fake-orgasm scene that was filmed at the table. But real ecstasy will come from eating the food. Katz's Delicatessen is a popular lunchtime spot, with a line that snakes out the front door and down Ludlow Street. Here, the food, the atmosphere, and the history are unique. Getting in can be as difficult as going through a security check at the airport. At the entrance, you must take a ticket and wait for the counterperson to call your number. Do not lose your ticket or you have to start the process over! The deli has been in so many movies that you will recognize it instantly. The long counter along the entire right side of the restaurant looks more like a conveyor belt in a large meat factory. There are men in white paper hats carving slabs of pastrami with the dexterity of surgeons. And the food flies off the counter at lightning speed. Katz's Deli is world-renowned. They've been serving their own pastrami since opening in 1888, and the sandwich is juicy, fresh, savory, and mouth-watering. The hot dogs with mustard and sauerkraut alone are worth the trip. In addition to eating at the restaurant—a not-to-be-missed, one-of-a-kind New York experience—you can buy everything here to go, so you can re-create Katz's at home. Don't be put off by the crowds: You don't want to miss one of the great treats in New York City. **5**

KOSSAR'S BIALYS

Most people have never seen or eaten a bialy, a chewy, yeasty roll covered with onions. It has its origins in the Jewish community of Bialystok, about a hundred miles northwest of Warsaw. That community was destroyed in the Holocaust, but the tradition of *bialystoker kuchen* continues today at Kossar's. The dough, or *tagelach*—made of high-gluten flour, yeast, and water—is molded by hand into a distinctive saucer shape, then coated with onion paste made from freshly cut onions. The raw bialys are baked on wooden "peels" in a special brick oven for seven minutes. Always buy bialys hot, and always buy them at Kossar's. Slathered with cream cheese, the taste is indescribable. **6**

GRAPEFRUIT WITH CAMPARI SORBET

Il Laboratorio del Gelato

SERVES 4

This icy treat is so refreshing it could serve as an appetizer before a summer meal.

- 2 cups freshly squeezed grapefruit juice
- ⅓ cup sugar
- 2 tablespoons Campari

Combine the grapefruit juice, sugar, and Campari with ¼ cup water in a lidded bottle and shake until the sugar is completely dissolved. Freeze in an ice-cream maker according to the manufacturer's directions.

7

7

IL LABORATORIO DEL GELATO

The genius behind Il Laboratorio del Gelato is Jon Snyder, a man with a passion for ice cream and a flair for marketing. As a teenager, Snyder worked in his family's Carvel business, and then went on to create Ciao Bella Gelato, a boutique brand he later sold. After a short stint in banking, Jon started Il Laboratorio del Gelato, an experimental ice-cream "lab," to try out new flavors and consistencies. As scientific as this may sound, the gelato here is clearly the work of artisans—dense, creamy, and delicious. Early in the morning, at his first shop on Ludlow Street, passersby could see Jon through the window receiving shipments of fresh fruits, herbs, and produce while working on small batches of gelato for all the top New York restaurants. A few years ago, Snyder moved to a larger space to expand his retail operation. You can now pick from almost two hundred gelato and sorbet flavors. Although Snyder travels the world searching for unique ingredients, he likes to source locally as well. The apple sorbet comes in green, Fuji, Gala, Braeburn, and Honeycrisp flavors; the grape is available in black, Concord, green, and red versions, and all are made from fruits grown in New York state. Il Laboratorio is a required pilgrimage for any gelato aficionado or, if you are curious but not quite so adventuresome, sample any one of the twelve varieties of chocolate sorbet. The intense "research and development" of Il Laboratorio shows in every spoonful; this is some of the finest ice cream you will taste anywhere in the world. **7**

MELT

In between the few traditional stores that are left on Orchard Street, standing like a beacon between a fur coat store and a bridal shop, is Melt, the coolest ice-cream store on the planet. It's one of many original food establishments that have come to the Lower East Side.

Ice-cream sandwiches have been popular for quite a long time, but Melt does not sell your run-of-the-mill slice of ice cream between two waffles or cookies. When Julian Plyter, a pastry chef, and Kareem Hamedy decided to create the best ice-cream sandwiches on earth, they focused on quality ingredients and the process. It takes them about three days to make their version, but it's out of this world. At Melt both the ice cream and the cookies are made from scratch each morning. Once the ice cream is frozen, it's scooped to fit between two cookies and the ice-cream sandwiches are frozen again. On day three, they're ready: the most creamy, decadent ice-cream sandwiches you've ever sunk your teeth into.

They come in two sizes and more than fifty flavors. You can order them in advance or stop by the store. Try to come in the morning when the cookies are baking—the unforgettable aroma of the warm dough will carry you away. **8**

THE PICKLE GUYS

In the eighteenth century, cucumbers were ferried from Brooklyn to Manhattan to be made into pickles. Because pickles did well without refrigeration, they became a staple food for poor immigrant families. At one time there were more than one hundred pickle stores in New York City. After the departure of Guss' Pickles, The Pickle Guys hold the distinction of being the last pickle shop in the neighborhood, and the facade harkens back to the golden age of pickles on the Lower East Side.

The briny aroma fills the store, but sadly the old-fashioned wooden barrels have been replaced by red plastic. There are easily fifty different types of pickles: horseradish, sweet gherkins, half sour, and hot sour, as well as tomatillos, sun-dried tomatoes, garlic-stuffed olives, pimiento olives, whole green olives, peperoncini, and pickled habanero peppers, celery, carrots, grape tomatoes, garlic, sweet peppers, string beans, okra . . . in other words, a pickle to please any palate. As in the past, you can buy half-pints or pints, quarts, half-gallons or gallons, or just grab a pickle to go. **9**

8

9

9

RUSS & DAUGHTERS

"I'm going to the appetizing" is pure New York–ese for a store that sells the best smoked fish, caviar, cheese, bagels, and other eastern European delicacies. Without question, the most appetizing of these stores is Russ & Daughters, in business since 1904. A third generation of the Russ family opened the Houston Street store in 1940. The neon sign seems lifted from an Edward Hopper painting. As you enter Russ & Daughters, you are welcomed into another world. The white enamel counters and cases are pristine dioramas for the sparkling array of delicacies: several kinds of Nova, fresh sturgeon, sable, white fish, smoked salmon, battalions of cream cheeses in assorted flavors, and pickled herring, olives, homemade egg salad, and tuna. If you want to start a new ritual, head to Russ & Daughters on December 31 and join the block-long line of loyal customers waiting patiently in the cold for a chance to buy a few ounces of caviar to ring in the New Year. **10**

THE SWEET LIFE

Siblings Sam Greenfield and Diane Miller bought The Sweet Life in 2004 and stocked it to capacity with as many salty and sweet things as they could find. The store motto is "Anything can be dipped in chocolate," and the assortment of treats is mind-boggling. The chocolate-dipped marshmallows rolled in M&M's are a big hit, but if that does not strike your fancy, you can try chocolate-dipped apricot, oranges, caramel apples, and raisins, among other treats. The center of the store is a smorgasbord of dried fruits and nuts, just begging you to take a taste (and you can do so). Greenfield manages to find the biggest and the freshest examples of everything—papaya bits, crystallized ginger, organic dried mango—sourced from all over the word. If it's licorice you seek, there are about twenty-five choices, but our favorite sweet here is the milk chocolate Oreo bark. The Sweet Life is a sweetheart of a candy store. **11**

YONAH SCHIMMEL KNISH BAKERY

Well before fast food, there was Yonah Schimmel's knishery, founded in 1910. The knish is a handheld Jewish dumpling, a pierogi offshoot, with a thin dough wrapped around a soft filling, usually mashed potatoes or kasha (buckwheat), or sometimes spinach, and then steamed or grilled until smoking hot. In eastern Europe, knishes were quite small, but in New York they evolved to the size of a shotput ball and are often just as heavy. But at Yonah Schimmel, the knishes are pillowy froths of flavor surrounded by delicate pastry. Buy a few boxes of knishes to keep in your freezer at home. **12**

LOWER MANHATTAN

Lower Manhattan—encompassing Tribeca, the financial district, and South Street Seaport—is the center of global finance and the site of the Staten Island ferry docks, and has the best view of the Statue of Liberty in town. It is also a real estate mecca. The area is lively all day long and very quiet at night.

By now, most of the wholesale markets have moved to the Hunts Point market in the Bronx and a variety of smaller, more unique stores have moved in. The restaurants are charming and there are merchants selling everything from pet supplies to wine.

Tribeca became the trendiest place to live for young couples with children and bank and finance men and women who love the idea of living in a loft near work. The Financial District is invaded every morning by hordes of bankers and tourists ogling 1 World Trade Center. Vendors sell souvenirs and there is a cornucopia of food trucks selling everything from frozen yogurt to beef on a stick. It is possible to stay downtown all day and definitely shop till you drop, eat till you can't, and look at some of the most amazing architecture. The Seaport buildings, although changing by the minute, are the only remnants left of this historic part of New York. There is definitely an invasion of new and fun foodstuffs at the Seaport, side by side with Tribeca's population, which shops at Whole Foods and gets deliveries from Fresh Direct. The Financial District is about to host a new giant Vesey Market, interspersed with smaller interesting stores and, of course, the ever-present food trucks.

ARCADE BAKERY

The hardest bakery to find in New York is Arcade Bakery, which is hidden from street view in the gorgeous lobby of the Merchants Square building at 220 Church Street in Tribeca. There is a nondescript sign for the bakery on the building, but the aroma of baking bread and pizza will draw you in. The bakery can be accessed by walking through the lobby entrance adjacent to New York Law School. The arcade is only 1,000 square feet, but on any given day Roger Gural, the owner, and his team will feed an enormous crowd as they pass through the lobby on their way to the elevators. The aroma alone will make you stop and order just about anything on the menu!

Customers rave about the bread, the pizza, the croissants, and the brioche. It's hard to choose what to get—everything looks and smells incredible—but we settled on one of the individual pizzas and almost went back for a second. The bubbly, airy, crispy crust is out of this world. We devoured it. We also tried the croissants, and their flakiness and buttery taste would be a match for those of any French baker. **1**

LE DISTRICT

Le District is located in the Financial District in the new Brookfield Place at 225 Liberty Street, an upscale mall with familiar retail names and a giant food court, all facing a beautiful tree-adorned garden and, of course, the Hudson River. Choose something delicious to eat, take it to the promenade, find a bench, and watch the world float by or, better yet, walk into the aptly named Palm Court, grab a seat, and rest awhile under the palm trees.

Le District is found directly beneath the Hudson Eats food court. A large portion of Le District is occupied by a domino-like series of food stalls selling seafood, meat, fruits, vegetables, cheese, and flowers, as well as French crêpes made to order and delivered hot from the pan. There are counters with prepared foods, including sandwiches and rotisserie chicken; a memorable selection of charcuterie, including saucisses de Toulouse, saucisson, French ham, and bacon; and, to satisfy your sweet tooth, pastries, ice cream, and a wall of candy and cookies that would make Willy Wonka proud. So if you long for the taste of Paris but can't make the transatlantic trip, visit Le District: It will make you feel like you have. 2

PASANELLA & SON VINTNERS

It isn't easy for a new wine store to capture the attention of New Yorkers: Everyone already has a favorite. But Pasanella not only boasts the right goods, it has one of the most beautiful interiors of any wine merchant in the city. One of the oldest neighborhoods in New York City, the South Street Seaport was once home to the famous Fulton Fish Market. When this market moved to the Bronx, the seaport lost its energy. But because of the beautiful buildings going up and the new wave of people moving to Lower Manhattan, the seaport is experiencing a resurgence—and this wine store is definitely one of the draws.

After September 11, Marco Pasanella and his wife, Rebecca Robertson, an interior designer and former editor at *Martha Stewart Living*, bought a small building and renovated it to perfection. Walk in and take a look around: This isn't just a wine store but an homage to times past. The interior is laden with history, from the brick walls to the vintage floors. It has been renovated with taste, flair, and a respect for the building itself. You almost feel like you are going back in time. The tasting room, which has thirteen-foot ceilings and opens up to a garden in the back, was once a large refrigerator for salmon sold at the Fulton Fish Market. The walls throughout are covered with personal collections, all equally eye-catching. You almost forget that you came here to buy wine. But the shop stocks an impressive selection of more than four hundred wines, ranging from wines produced by small family-run vineyards to those from the most well-respected and sought-after wine makers, including a wide selection of bottles for under fifteen dollars. Every bottle in the store has been hand-selected, along with the adorable Fiat you'll see as you enter (used for deliveries). Make the trip: It is more than worth it to buy even just a bottle or two. **3**

ZUCKER'S BAGELS & SMOKED FISH

In the middle of Chambers Street, one of the busiest streets in Tribeca, stands Zucker's, a delicatessen oasis in a sea of totally unrelated businesses. You will have to wait on line to choose your bagel, but this gives you time to pick from the endless list of choices written on a chalkboard on the back wall. It is a veritable mural of words beckoning you to change your mind three or four times, as the options all sound delicious. Order your bagel with a smear of cream cheese and some Nova, and a slice of tomato and onion, and you will be in bagel heaven.

Matt Pomerantz, one of the owners, was working on Wall Street when he decided he wanted to start an old-time kosher deli. With no knowledge about how to make bagels and an unreliable bagel-machine operator, he decided to hire somebody to hand-roll and kettle-boil the bagels. The bagels became an instantaneous success and have been referred to as some of the best bagels in the city. Zucker's hand-rolled bagels are crisp on the outside, chewy on the inside, and completely memorable. If you are passionate about bagels, this is the place to test your loyalties. And if you're an out-of-towner who's never had an authentic New York bagel, this would be a good place to try your first. Zucker's carries more than a dozen kinds of smoked fish, as well as corned beef, pastrami, and salads that will knock your taste buds into the stratosphere. It's an epicurean delight, morning, noon, and afternoon. **4**

MIDTOWN

Midtown is the commercial heart of the city, twenty square blocks packed with skyscraping corporate headquarters and flagship stores displaying the world's famous fashion brands. Midtown is home to the New York Public Library, the Museum of Modern Art, the Empire State Building, Radio City Music Hall, and the Broadway theater district. The streets here buzz with energy day and night. Midtown also houses some of the most prestigious restaurants and food stores in Manhattan. Taking a cue from the world of fashion, many of the leading food brands have opened flagship stores in Midtown. But as you head farther west or south, you'll find smaller, less established food stores every bit as interesting as their more corporate neighbors. In between Fortieth and Fifty-Ninth Streets, west of Eighth Avenue, there's the gentrified Hell's Kitchen, which was once the turf of the toughest gangs in New York. Now the neighborhood has been renamed Clinton. Its side streets are home to an unusual mix of food shops and restaurants. Another Midtown enclave, Koreatown, centers on Thirty-Second Street between Broadway and Fifth Avenue. The block is dense with Korean restaurants, karaoke bars, and other unidentified haunts, and, of course, some amazing food stores. Koreatown booms at night as many places stay open late. It's worth visiting just to see all the lights alone. So after a Broadway matinee or in between visits to dressing rooms in Barney's, Gucci, or Saks, check out some of the amazing food stores in this neighborhood.

AMY'S BREAD

After studying at the French Culinary Institute and Bouley Bakery, Amy Schreiber went to France and learned the art of baking bread from the masters. But when she opened her first bakery in Hell's Kitchen more than twenty years ago, the reputation of the neighborhood was such that people told her she'd be better off opening a shop in the Balkans. But Schreiber is a courageous woman, and her store eventually became the cornerstone of the Hell's Kitchen renaissance. It will soon expand into the space next door, as the original space cannot fulfill the popular demand of her loyal customers and her catering business. Amy's Bread is also a thriving wholesale business with an operation in Long Island City, but Schreiber has held on to her original vision: to offer New Yorkers world-class fresh-baked bread, pastries, brownies, cookies, and cupcakes.

The excellence of Amy's abounds: Every day they bake bread from more than twenty different doughs in various shapes and sizes. If you have room for only one Amy's item, you are in trouble: We could not choose between the prosciutto–black pepper bread, the granola, the fig and olive stick, and the signature semolina bread with golden raisins and fennel, so we bought several items and shared. **1**

BOUCHON BAKERY

Bouchon Bakery in Manhattan (the original is in northern California) is part of the Thomas Keller restaurant empire. Located at the Time Warner Center, one floor below Keller's restaurant Per Se, Bouchon Bakery has an enviable view of Central Park West and shows off some of the most delicious and beautifully crafted pastries in New York City. The retail counter for takeout is reminiscent of an old French patisserie; the white tile, bread racks, and marble counters will transport you to Paris. If you are not in a hurry, buy a pastry and a coffee and watch the world go by. Nicholas Bonamico presides over the nuanced production of everything from the croissants to the handcrafted tarts and pastries. The éclairs at Bouchon are our favorite—light, airy, and filled with delectable pastry cream. Each flavor is unique, but the dulce de leche is a must. **2**

BURGUNDY WINE

Bordeaux is easy. Burgundy is hard. Burgundy Wine is an entire store dedicated to the greatness of the big Pinot Noirs. While Bordeaux proceeds in orderly fashion, from St.-Émilion to Pomerol, vintage to vintage and château to château, the wines of Burgundy are ever-so-slightly organized chaos. The nomenclature is convoluted, a hodgepodge of regions, towns, hillsides, and terroirs. Sometimes just a couple of hectares make a big difference, which makes mastering the wines of Burgundy a challenge. In most wine stores, your questions about Burgundy will get less-than-informed answers. At Burgundy Wine the mission is to make these great wines accessible to a wider audience. This is the place to learn about Côte de Nuit, Côte de Beaune, Volney, Gevrey Chambertin, Chambolle Musigny, La Tâche, or Puligny Montrachet. Bottles are neatly arranged by region, and the staff will take the time to pick wines that match your meal. 3

OEUFS EN MEURETTE
(POACHED EGGS IN RED WINE SAUCE)
Burgundy Wine Company

SERVES 4

Eggs Benedict are familiar; *oeufs en meurette* not as much. In this version we replace the English muffins with *croûtes*—a sliced, buttered, and grilled baguette, which adds some crispness to the dish.

½ pound bacon or pancetta, diced
1 onion, thinly sliced
1 tablespoon tomato paste
1 (750-ml) bottle red Burgundy
1 cup brown veal stock
Salt and freshly ground black pepper
2 tablespoons unsalted butter
1 baguette, cut into 1-inch-thick slices
1 tablespoon white vinegar
8 large eggs

1 In a pan, sauté the bacon until golden. Drain the fat from the pan and add the onion and tomato paste. Cook for about 10 minutes over medium heat, stirring occasionally, until lightly browned. Add the wine, reduce the heat to low, and simmer until the sauce has reduced to about 2 cups. Add the brown veal stock and reduce to 2 cups over medium-low heat. Season the sauce with salt and pepper.

2 Butter the baguette slices and toast them in a preheated 350°F oven until browned and crunchy.

3 When you're ready to poach the eggs, prepare a bowl of ice and water. In a deep pot, bring 4 cups salted water and the vinegar to a boil. Crack one egg into a dish. Reduce the heat of the boiling water to a simmer and create a whirlpool by stirring clockwise. Drop the egg into the center of the whirlpool and cook for 2 minutes or until firm enough to remove to the ice water with a slotted spoon. Repeat with the remaining seven eggs.

4 To assemble, bring the wine sauce to a low simmer. Arrange the *croûtes* on a baking sheet. Top each *croûte* with one poached egg. Heat in the oven at 350°F for 3 minutes. Plate the *croûtes*/eggs and generously ladle wine sauce over them. Serve immediately.

ESPOSITO MEAT MARKET

With its neon signs and various meats hanging from a rack in the window, Esposito Meat Market reflects the vanishing scene of the old-fashioned New York butcher. They haven't moved from this corner since 1932; Robert, a grandson of the founder, Giovanni Esposito, is responsible for continuing the family legacy on Ninth Avenue. If you need a whole suckling pig for Christmas or a lamb for Easter, these orders and more can be filled within twenty-four hours. This family-run butcher has been a West Side favorite for more than eighty years. The men in their white coats will give you cooking tips and coach you through the cuts of meat with charm and a smile. Esposito is known for its pork, so much so that it manufactures ten thousand pounds of sausage each week. Make sure you don't go home without purchasing some of the house-made links, such as the hot or sweet Italian varieties. **4**

GRAND CENTRAL MARKET

Grand Central Market, located in Grand Central Terminal, has a potential customer base of about 750,000 daily commuters from New York's Westchester, Putnam, and Dutchess Counties, and Connecticut. Shopping at this glorious market before returning home to the suburbs is a must. There is magnificent food at every turn and almost every wish for a great meal—breakfast, lunch, or dinner—can be fulfilled. Pescatore offers a full array of fresh seafood; the Murray's Cheese outpost has a vast selection of cheese, crackers, olives, and meats; Ceriello is an Italian butcher and specialty shop; Spices and Tease offers spices and spice blends, salts, and herbs; at Eli Zabar's find breads, pastries, fruits, and vegetables; and, last but not least, Li-Lac Chocolates has the perfect finishing touch to your meal (or shopping trip, if you can't wait). If you've spent a tough day at the office—any office—and you're ready to retreat to Greenwich or even Greenwich Village, buy your family dinner here and avoid that second commute to the local supermarket. **5**

CRISPY CHICKEN WINGS

Grand Central Market

MAKES ABOUT 50 WINGS

These wings are baked, not fried, so they are less fattening and definitely not as messy but just as crispy and tasty. Serve with blue cheese salad dressing and celery sticks for dipping.

FOR THE BUFFALO SAUCE

1 tablespoon unsalted butter

¼ cup hot sauce, such as Frank's

¼ teaspoon cayenne pepper

¼ teaspoon freshly ground black pepper

¼ teaspoon kosher salt

FOR THE WINGS

5 pounds chicken wings and drumettes, separated and tips removed

FOR THE SOY-GINGER GLAZE

1½ cups honey

3 tablespoons soy sauce

2 cloves garlic, crushed

1 (2-inch) piece fresh ginger, peeled and finely sliced

1 Preheat the oven to 400°F. Set wire racks inside two large rimmed baking sheets to catch any drips.

MAKE THE BUFFALO SAUCE WINGS

2 Melt the butter in a small saucepan. Add the rest of the Buffalo sauce ingredients, stirring until warm and well combined. Pour the warm sauce into a large bowl, add the wings, and toss until they're thoroughly coated. Divide the wings between the prepared racks and spread out in a single layer. Bake for 50 to 60 minutes, until the wings are cooked through and the skin is crispy. Do not turn off the oven.

MAKE THE SOY-GINGER-GLAZED WINGS

3 Line another rimmed baking sheet with foil and place a wire rack in the pan. In another large bowl, whisk together the ingredients for the soy-ginger glaze. Add half of the crispy wings to the soy-ginger glaze and arrange them in a single layer on the wire rack. Bake until the wings are glazed and caramelized, about 10 to 15 minutes.

INTERNATIONAL GROCERY

The facade of this Ninth Avenue grocery store is unprepossessing, but as soon as you walk in you are steeped in the ambiance of an Istanbul souk. The burlap sacks are bursting with the colors of a Persian rug; the red, orange, and yellow of the dried peas, lentils, and beans give the feeling of the sun about to rise. The music, the old television, the display of spices, beans, couscous, flour, olives, and feta cheese all are reminiscent of a market in Morocco. Some customers come here exclusively for the olive oil sold by the gallon, and swear by the quality and price. Others come for the variety of spices and nuts, which are always very fresh, or the selection of Greek foods—taramasalata, feta cheese, dried oregano, and sumac all can be found here. This is international at its best, and no passport is needed. **6**

KALUSTYAN'S

If spice was still used as currency, Kalustyan's could be the Federal Reserve. Founded in 1944, Kalustyan's is the largest retail spice dealer in New York City. They supply most of the great restaurants, but they will gladly sell you a few ounces or a few hundred pounds of any spice on your list. The store's product offerings have expanded, so alongside Asian and Indian spices, you will find Arborio rice from Italy; green lentils from France; and olive oil from Greece. In fact, the store carries 190 different types of rice and more than 90 different varieties of dals and lentils. You will also find salt from the Himalayas, chutneys from southern India, and pistachios from Iran. Kalustyan's provides a full list of products on its website, but don't pass up a visit to this remarkable store, one of those magical places in New York where you can shop with your nose. **7**

LA BOÎTE

Spices have always been associated with exotic countries. Luckily, chef Lior Lev Sercarz, creator of La Boîte, has opened a library of spices, sandwiched between an auto-repair garage and a fenced-in corner garden on the far west side of Manhattan, that's beloved by foodies and chefs from around the country. Sercarz has the charming looks of a mad composer and he possesses a huge repertoire of information. He is a magician of sorts who, with a flick of his wrist, can change the way we season all our food, from a simple omelet to a complex meat dish or even a scoop of ice cream.

The shop, which features more than forty custom spice blends plus salts and peppers that elevate the flavors of ordinary chicken, fish, or steak to unknown heights, is open to the public only twelve hours a week. Visit when you're not in a rush; Sercarz will patiently explain everything in the store and then some. In addition to his spices, Sercarz offers a very tasty selection of seasonal biscuits inspired by methods and ingredients used by cultures around the world. They are sweet with savory notes, incorporating dried fruits, nuts, olive oil, and spices, and packaged in collectible tins decorated by artists Sercarz commissions twice a year. All the biscuits can be served with cheese or as dessert. **8**

MICHEL CLUIZEL

When Marcelle and Marc Cluizel started their chocolate journey in northern France in 1948, they had no idea that one day they would be one of the largest independent producers of fine chocolate—from bean to finished bar—in the world, with a store on Lexington Avenue and a factory in New Jersey. The company owns five plantations, has developed chocolate with a unique aroma, and has recently launched an "Ingredients Noble" label to highlight the quality of cocoa, sugar, and vanilla used in their products. We always buy chocolate squares, truffles, caramel and hazelnut chocolate in the shape of a mushroom, and the foil-wrapped chocolate sardines in a tin can. Marc, Michel's son and the grandson of Marcelle and Marc, is now at the helm of the family chocolate business. **9**

MINAMOTO KITCHOAN

At this pristine Japanese shop, baking and wrapping is an art form. A Zen-like calm pervades the minimalist space, underscored by Japanese music playing softly. The miniature cakes, exquisitely decorated, reside under glass. There is so much artistry in these confections, each likely to disappear in one bite, that they speak volumes about the devotion of the bakers. The shapes, the names, and the ingredients take some time to learn, but the shopkeepers go out of their way to help you understand the offerings, all traditional Japanese pastries made from a base of rice flour, bean jam, and sugar.

Some of our favorites are *uguisu-mochi*, sweet red beans wrapped in rice cake and a green pea flour coating, and *mamedaifuku*, sweet red beans wrapped in rice cake with red peas. There is also a tasty marzipan made with bean paste instead of almonds. A silk screen on the right side of the shop changes according to the season, and the flavors, featuring seasonal fruits and nuts, also change. In spring, try the cherry blossom flavor; in summer, the Japanese fruit gelatin and sorbets. In the fall, we sampled the chestnut, and in the winter, the unusual and delicious cakes made from sweet potato. All are a memorable visual and taste experience. **10**

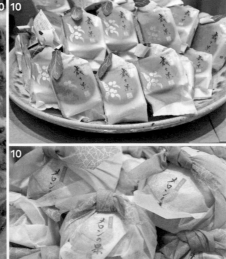

PETROSSIAN

In one of the great ironies of the Russian Revolution, it was the spartan Bolsheviks who introduced the pleasures of caviar to the decadent French. Leon Trotsky, at the head of the Red Army, drove thousands of upper-class Russians across the border and eventually into France. These émigrés—"white Russians"—brought along their taste for smoked salmon, sturgeon, and sturgeon eggs, also known as caviar. In the 1920s, Paris fell under the spell of these new émigrés.

Over the decades, the Petrossian brothers' little corner store on Paris's Avenue Motte Piquet grew into the largest importer and processor of caviar in the world. Luckily, the Petrossian family is still importing and selling caviar today. The New York store is run by Alexandre Petrossian, great-grandson of the founder, and housed in the historic Alwyn Court Building, just one block from Carnegie Hall. It offers some of the world's finest ossetra, beluga, Siberian, Alverta, and Shassetra caviar. Petrossian also sells smoked and cured salmon, foie gras, and truffles, as well as chocolates and a bakery featuring baba au rum, croissants, cakes, and tartlets, that complete any meal organized around the caviar. And, of course, there are blinis and crème fraîche. But if you're a purist, just enjoy a mother-of-pearl spoonful. **11**

POSEIDON BAKERY

Once upon a time, Greek bakeries, restaurants, and groceries lined the stretch of Ninth Avenue between Forty-Fourth and Forty-Fifth Streets. Today, Poseidon Bakery, founded in 1923 by Demetrios Anagnostou, is the sole survivor. This authentic Greek pastry shop—with its blue-and-white facade and neon lights—is run by the same family and still sells its pastries straight from the tin molds in which they were baked.

Don't miss the spinach and feta spanakopita, a Greek-style empanada, or the *kreatopita*, a meat pie, the fillings wrapped in crisp phyllo dough. You can also purchase frozen hors d'oeuvres to take home, or make your own from the first-rate fresh phyllo dough made by hand right on the premises. *Kourambiedes*, the Greek cookies traditionally baked for the New Year, are available here year-round. The butter cookies, made with crushed almonds and rolled in powdered sugar, are wonderful with espresso. But our favorite is the baklava, layer upon layer of phyllo laced with chopped walnuts and dripping with honey. **12**

SULLIVAN STREET BAKERY

Jim Lahey started Sullivan Street Bakery more than twenty years ago, and although they moved from their Soho location to larger quarters in Hell's Kitchen in 2000, the name is still the same. While living in Italy, Lahey studied to be a sculptor before learning the art of bread making, but looking at the beautiful breads his bakery produces, it is apparent that sculpting plays a part. Sullivan Street Bakery has been home to the best bread baked in the city since it opened its doors in 1994.

The signature Pugliese has a dark, crispy exterior with a soft, spongy interior, perfect for dipping in olive oil or sweet butter. The raisin walnut loaf is packed with whole grains, nuts, and raisins and is delicious toasted. The pizzas are works of art and just as tasty as the bread. There are six options, but the pizza bianca is our favorite: six feet long, with olive oil, sea salt, and rosemary. But there's more than bread and pizza here, such as the bombolini, the signature Italian doughnut made from a pillowy dough filled with a vanilla bean custard. Buy several loaves of bread and freeze them to have on hand; once you've tried them, you'll be coming back for more. Or, if you're the adventurous type, buy the cookbook and try your hand at replicating the recipes at home. **13**

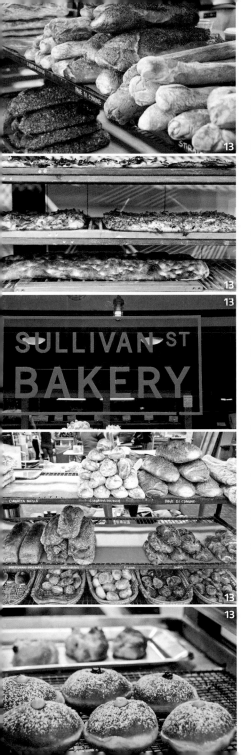

TOUS LES JOURS

A visit to Koreatown, on Thirty-Second Street between Broadway and Fifth Avenue, is always an experience: This block is bustling from dawn to dawn. Tous les Jours is a New York bakery with a French-Asian flair and is one of the most visited establishments on the block. There is a café in the back where you can sit and enjoy a delicious and visually beautiful array of cakes, interesting flavors of ice cream, crusty bread, and teas while listening to loud Korean rap. The pastries and breads are displayed cafeteria style, except for the exquisite whole cakes in the glass cases.

We took our time to look at everything; trust us, even after you do so, it is hard to decide. We finally chose an assortment: almond croissant, milk pan bread, honey pancake bread . . . and enjoyed every bite. So take a tray, walk around slowly to examine all your options, and then decide you cannot go wrong, as everything looks delicious. And, if you grew up in the era of Wonder Bread, an American staple, the bakery's fluffy white bread will give you new ideas about what white bread can be. **14**

SOHO

Soho, the neighborhood just south of Houston Street, spreads south to Canal Street and east from Hudson Street to Lafayette Street. The area we call Soho began as a nameless neighborhood of factories and warehouses lodged in beautifully proportioned, nineteenth-century cast-iron buildings, many of which were land-marked in the 1970s. In the late sixties and early seventies, swarms of young artists were lured to Soho by low rents; they turned the huge factory loft spaces into illegal live-in studios. Throughout the eighties and nineties, fashion followed art, and the bare lofts, now legitimized, became magnificent homes for the trendy and famous. At store level, funky plumbing supply companies, Old-World family fabric businesses, and suppliers of leather goods for the shoe trade gave way to some of the world's most luxurious boutiques and res-taurants. Rem Koolhaas designed Prada's new flagship store at the corner of Broadway and Prince. Magnates of media, fashion, and finance now pay millions to live in what used to be shoe factories.

But for us, it's the food stores that make Soho exciting—they're as authentic as the architecture and as diverse as the Sunday crowds. No matter where you are in Soho, you're always just a few steps away from some of New York's most remarkable food boutiques.

BALTHAZAR BAKERY

Proust had his madeleines to take him back to lost times, and denizens of Soho have their own pâtisserie time machine. As you enter Balthazar Bakery, breathe in the earthy smell of baking bread and pastry, then look around: You're in France, the year is 1910, and the place, a corner boulangerie. The crusty baguette here is tasty enough to pass the toughest Parisian muster. The airy brioche dissolves in the deep, dark coffee. The buttery, crisp croissants, in happy contrast to the leaden crescents New Yorkers have put up with for years, seem to float on the plate. The miche, a round, hard-crusted bread with the Balthazar "B" embossed on the side, is perfect for rough slicing into a hearty breakfast tartine. And the much-revered chocolate bread is incomparable. At Balthazar Bakery, antique silver-leafed mirrors and old cases speak of the past, but the baked goods here are present perfect. **1**

DEAN & DELUCA

Dean & DeLuca, which started in the late seventies as Giorgio DeLuca's tiny cheese store on Prince Street, has grown into a high-end theme park for food lovers in a landmark building on Broadway. White-coated salespeople preside over this soaring, white-columned, marble-floored expanse dedicated to the proposition that when it comes to food, more is better: more choice, more variety, and more quality. On shimmering stainless-steel racks, in glistening glass cases, in barrels and urns, in tureens and on trays, you'll find the finest meats, fish, chocolate, pastry, caviar, sturgeon, charcuterie, truffles, prepared food, candies, cakes, syrups, jams, and bread. Shopping for mustard? You will find varieties from France, England, Sweden, and Germany. Buying olives here is a geography lesson: kalamata, gaeta, Basque, lucque, Catalan, Casablanca mixed, Provençal, cigniopia, castelvetrano, picholine. With more than sixty different oils (thirty of which are olive) and thirty-seven different varieties of vinegar, the possibilities for salad dressing alone are infinite. George Bernard Shaw wrote, "There is no love sincerer than the love of food." It's clear that Dean & DeLuca not only loves food, but champions its customers' love of the same. **2**

DOMINIQUE ANSEL BAKERY

If you like to wait in line at five o'clock in the morning, you have two options in Soho: either go to the Apple Store on Prince Street to purchase the latest device, or head to Dominique Ansel Bakery to get a couple of Cronuts when the store opens at eight a.m. Before masterminding the Cronut (the croissant-doughnut hybrid), Dominique Ansel was already a well-known pastry chef. He began his career working for Chef Daniel Boulud, then moved on to open his own bakery. If you are not one for waiting in line and do not have the urge for the trendy Cronut, Ansel also makes a Custard Canelé, a traditional dessert from Bordeaux that looks like a castle turret; Ansel stuffs his with a mouth-watering custard cream. Or, for a fresh take on milk and cookies, you could order a round of shots: chocolate chip cookies baked in a shot glass shape and filled with chilled organic milk. Bottoms up! However, if you are singlemindedly obsessed with his Cronuts, you can order them online at cronutpreorder.com. Online preordering enables you to order a maximum of six instead of the two you are allowed to purchase at the bakery (even after waiting in line for an hour or two). **3**

4

FRANÇOIS PAYARD BAKERY

François Payard is a James Beard Award–winning pastry chef who grew up in the French Riviera town of Nice, where he learned the techniques of classic French pastry at an early age in his grandfather's shop. Many years, four-star ratings, and culinary awards later, he opened Payard Patisserie in 1997. In 2010, he moved from that original, much-loved Upper East Side location to Soho and christened the new spot FPB (short for François Payard Bakery). As you might expect from such an esteemed chef, the breakfast pastries are in a league of their own. The classic French morning breads—butter croissants, almond croissants, and pains aux chocolats—will give you an idea of the standards this man upholds. The scones and muffins will impress the most demanding customers, and the pastries and tarts, which look almost too good to eat, are exquisite. The signature cake selection includes Le Gateau Roulé, a light rolled cake in flavors such as chocolate raspberry, milk chocolate espresso, hazelnut, and passion fruit cheesecake. Or try the French version of angel food cake, called Le Lorrain. Payard's croquembouche, a tower of profiteroles filled with vanilla, chocolate, coffee, kirsch, or vanilla rum cream and finished with hand-pulled sugar ribbons, is nothing less than legendary. *Merci beaucoup*, Monsieur Payard! 4

FLOURLESS CHOCOLATE COOKIES

From the kitchen of François Payard, a French legend on the New York food scene.

MAKES TWELVE 4-INCH COOKIES

½ cup plus 3 tablespoons unsweetened Dutch-processed
   cocoa powder
3 cups confectioners' sugar
Pinch of salt
2¾ cups walnuts, toasted and coarsely chopped
4 large egg whites, at room temperature
1 tablespoon pure vanilla extract

1 Preheat the oven to 350°F and arrange racks in the upper and lower thirds of the oven. Line two baking sheets with parchment paper or silicone baking mats.

2 In the bowl of an electric mixer fitted with the paddle attachment, combine the cocoa powder, confectioners' sugar, salt, and walnuts. Mix on low speed for 1 minute. With the mixer running, gradually add the egg whites and vanilla. Beat on medium speed for 3 minutes, until the mixture has thickened slightly; do not overmix, or the egg whites will thicken too much.

3 Using a 2-ounce cookie or ice-cream scoop or a large spoon, scoop the dough onto the prepared baking sheets to make cookies that are 4 inches in diameter; scoop about five cookies onto each pan, about 3 inches apart, so they won't stick to one another when they spread. If you have extra dough, wait until the first batch of cookies is baked before scooping the next batch.

4 Put the cookies in the oven and immediately lower the oven temperature to 320°F. Bake for 14 to 16 minutes or until small, thin cracks appear on the surface of the cookies, rotating the pans between upper and lower racks halfway through baking.

5 Lift the parchment paper with the cookies onto a wire rack and let cool completely before removing the cookies from the paper. Store in an airtight container for up to 2 days.

5

GEORGETOWN CUPCAKE

Sisters Katherine Kallinis Berman and Sophie Kallinis LaMontagne are the cofounders of Georgetown Cupcakes and best-selling authors of the cookbooks *The Cupcake Diaries* and *Sweet Celebrations*.

This bakery makes the perfect cupcake: It has just the right ratio of cake to frosting, which is beautifully perched on the top. The selection of flavors listed on a board will entice you, and the display of cupcakes will send your taste buds into a whirl. Their perfect box designs house two, four, six, or eight of these lovely gems without shifting; they travel well and can be shipped overnight by FedEx. We loved the chocolate salted caramel flavor—a Valrhona chocolate cupcake with a dulce de leche core, topped with salted caramel buttercream frosting and a dulce de leche drizzle. The cookies and creme and the coconut cupcakes are also high on our list, but there is a flavor for every taste preference. **5**

6

GOURMET GARAGE

In Soho during the early eighties, it was a lot easier to find plumbing supplies, wholesale lingerie, or a Noguchi table than broccoli, potatoes, and a pound of ground beef for the evening's meat loaf. As more families moved into the neighborhood, it became clear that something very important was missing: an all-in-one food store with a selection of food sophisticated enough to please a discerning Soho appetite. So two neighborhood guys, Andy Arons and Adam Hartman, decided to open their own supermarket—and not just any supermarket, but a supermarket with a philosophy. Gourmet Garage brings Andy's idea to life. "Food is an international common denominator, and I wanted to demystify gourmet food and give it everyday appeal and pricing." Everything is simply stacked, contributing to a warehouse feel, but you are surrounded by gourmet food from all around the world. Along one aisle, you'll find an extensive array of breads; in the next, a global selection of packaged foods. The fruits and vegetables are flown in from six continents, and if anything grew on Antarctica, you'd probably find it here. At the new larger location on Broome Street, they kept the simple atmosphere but added a large salad bar, a sushi counter, a soup bar, and an extensive section of prepared food. Andy's motto is "Shop Like a Chef," and you will be treated like one here. **6**

HARNEY & SONS

John Harney is the patriarch of the Harney family, and the president and founder of Harney & Sons, a family company established in 1983 that's devoted to the tradition of fine teas. A master of tea blending, Harney & Sons is one of the world's most renowned tea companies, with more than two hundred gourmet teas on offer, sourced from China, Taiwan, India, Sri Lanka, Africa, and Japan. The Harney tradition of tea is simple—to make great tea an everyday luxury.

Harney & Sons opened their Soho tearoom in 2010, providing a Zen-like atmosphere for tasting tea and an education in the subject that you won't soon forget. The wall of shelves filled with tins of loose teas from around the world and their matching exotic names will give you pause for thought. The teas, the brewing paraphernalia, the sachets, the iced teas, and the friendly tutelage of the staff ensure that even if you weren't a tea drinker when you entered the store, you certainly will be by the time you leave. John Harney continues to serve as the quintessential brand ambassador and "tea-vangelist," spreading the everyday enjoyment of teas to the masses. **7**

KEE'S CHOCOLATES

Kee's was founded by Kee Ling Tong in 2002, after she quit her corporate job and followed her dream of making handmade chocolates. A small woman with the hands of a diamond setter, Kee makes thousands of her irresistible chocolates every week. She's the inventive genius behind all the confections and can be found in her shop daily. She creates the recipes, mixes the chocolate, makes the molds, stocks the displays, and serves the customers.

Kee uses only the freshest ingredients, sourced from all around the world, including yuzu from Japan, sea salt from France, and saffron from Spain. The flavors are seasonal, but there are over fifty chocolates to choose from—our favorites are the cherry cordial, the honey kumquat, the dark chocolate with ginger, and the chocolate truffles. She has now added macarons and chocolate bars to her repertoire, in addition to a fabulous selection of truffles. The artisan's touch is what makes Kee's Chocolates an essential stop during any visit to Soho. **8**

LADURÉE

This upscale Parisian pastry institution now has two locations in New York, thanks to Elisabeth Holder-Raberin and her husband, Pierre-Antoine Raberin, who have imported Ladurée perfection to the United States. Louis Ernest Ladurée's legacy is evident in the history, decor, culture, and pastries throughout the Ladurée empire. The first store, opened on the Rue Royale in Paris, in 1862, was a bakery, then a tea salon, before becoming a pastry shop. The store on Rue Bonapartre, designed by the renowned Madeleine Castaing, had a new flair. Pierre Desfontaines, a cousin of Louis Ernest, who decided to attach two macaron shells together with ganache, changed the course of macaron history and subsequently brought about the worldwide success of Ladurée. In the Soho shop, you can spend an hour just looking at the many macaron flavors—edible works of art perfectly displayed in their cases. The almost jewel-like pastries are also exquisite. Choose a box and a piece of ribbon from the display, have it filled with Ladurée pastries or confections, and you have an elegant gift for any occasion. In the spring and summer don't miss out on dining in the garden—one of the best alfresco locations in New York City.

As a young girl, Nathalie used to go to the Rue Royale Ladurée with her father on Saturday mornings. They would sit at a table downstairs and have a *croissant aux amandes*. Since her father passed away, she now takes her son, Lucien, once a week to Ladurée and lets him choose three macarons to enjoy. Visiting Ladurée regularly is a family experience they will continue to pass on from generation to generation. *Vive la France!* **9**

10

10

10

10

10

MARIEBELLE

Maribel Lieberman came to New York from Honduras more than twenty years ago, intending to start a career in fashion. She enrolled in Parsons School of Design, but her journey took a different turn. Instead she opened MarieBelle chocolates in Nolita in 2000, where she sold chocolates alongside fashion eyeglasses. MarieBelle is now ensconced on Broome Street in a classic cast-iron Soho building. The chocolates all feature an image on top and a legend in the box that explains each one. The fillings are seasonal and all are delicious and special. Sample the pistachio, Kona bean, peanut butter, ginger, lemon, espresso, pineapple, banana, caramel salt, cherry, coconut, matcha . . . and it doesn't stop there.

The first room in the shop houses the chocolate collection, the ice-cream bar, and cabinets filled with tins of cocoa, and assortments of chocolate bars, nuts, caramels, crisps, and gift boxes, containing from six to sixty pieces. The chocolate is made from Criollo cacao—one of the best types in the world; its flavor is rich, dense, and strong. The pièce de résistance is the second room, which possesses the feeling of an Old-World Parisian boudoir. Whether it's summer, winter, spring, or fall, escape to MarieBelle for some of the most heavenly chocolates in the world. And though there is never any reason to feel guilty about sampling Maribel's creations, studies demonstrate that the heart-healthy polyphenols found in dark chocolate are twice as powerful as the ones found in red wine. So enjoy every sip and every bite! If Maribel is in the shop when you are, meeting her is an even bigger treat. **10**

MARIEBELLE CHOCOLATE FONDUE

MarieBelle

SERVES 2

For all you fondue lovers, this is a spectacular recipe from Maribel Lieberman, owner of MarieBelle.

- ¾ cup MarieBelle shaved or powdered dark chocolate (70% cacao)
- ¼ cup boiling water
- Fresh seasonal fruit, cut into bite-size cubes or slices
- Confectioners' sugar, for dusting

Melt the chocolate in a bain marie over boiling water and whisk it with a spoon for a few seconds until silky and thick. Transfer the melted chocolate to a heat-resistant container with a tea candle underneath to keep the chocolate warm and soft. Skewer each piece of fruit on a wooden stick, dip into the chocolate, sprinkle with confectioners' sugar, and enjoy!

OLIVE'S

Soho was once an artists' haven, its warehouses more suitable for studios than commerce. Now it is as crowded as any neighborhood in the city, with visitors from all over the world. Husband-and-wife team Nick Hartman and Toni Allocca opened Olive's on Prince Street in 1992, with a mission to provide the people living in the area with delicious, freshly prepared foods to take away. These days, the line starts early in the morning for the freshly baked croissants, pain au chocolat, muffins, scones, and their famous Morning Buns—sticky cinnamon buns gooey beyond belief and finger-licking fantastic. However, the main event is the homemade cookies. The crisp but chewy chocolate chip cookies are so full of chips that each bite drips with chocolate—you'll need extra napkins! Other tasty options include oatmeal raisin, oatmeal pecan, peanut butter, and ginger. Olive's has some of the best cookies in town and the rest of their menu is pretty terrific, too! **11**

ONCE UPON A TART

Once Upon a Tart is a hidden jewel box. James Audereau opened this ode to sweet and savory tarts on Sullivan Street two decades ago, and it's still going strong with its new owners, chef Alicia Walter and her husband, Michael Stern, who have turned it into a full-service restaurant. From the vintage oak doors to the old-time feel of the interior and the freshly baked pastries, the place is a crowd-pleaser. Locals duly arrive in the morning for coffee and the signature scones and muffins. Walters also bakes sweet tarts, which resemble miniature pies, fresh daily. Big glass jars filled with various flavors of tempting biscotti are great for dipping into a hot cup of coffee. So what will it be? Choose among the items already mentioned or try a brownie, madeleine, macaron, or cookie. Our favorite is a slice of iced carrot cake because we love licking the icing off the ends of our fingers like we did when we were kids. Once Upon a Tart adds a new dimension to New York's gastronomic sweets, and it's so good that once you discover it . . . well, you just might want to keep it to yourself. **12**

PINO'S PRIME MEAT MARKET

The maestro of this old-school, Old-World butcher shop is Pino Cinquemani, who is still behind the counter every day after decades in business. There were five generations of Cinquemani butchers before Pino, and when he came to New York from Sicily he brought his family obsession with him: a passion for the perfect cut, which he has now passed on to his sons Sal and Leo. Pino believes that supplying the finest-quality beef, pork, and poultry—which he always does—is only the beginning. The real art is in the cutting, and here Pino is without peer. His steaks, chops, and roasts are perfectly proportioned, with just the right amount of fat and bone. A Pino's New York strip, cooked medium-rare is *bellissimo!* The Thanksgiving turkeys here are legendary, and every November pilgrims from up and down the East Coast trek to Pino's for their holiday bird. **13**

RAFFETTO'S

Raffetto's opened in 1906 on the now crowded West Houston Street, and this old-fashioned pasta store has managed to keep its original flair. The decor has barely changed, and the wooden display for the pasta is now a piece of history. In a neighborhood where we are used to the smell of fashion, Raffetto's infuses the air with the scent of garlic and tomatoes from the big pot of tomato sauce that slowly simmers on its stovetop.

Raffetto's is all about pasta—thin golden sheets of it rolled into crespelle, stripped into fettuccini, or hand-cut with amazing precision into cappellini or pappardelle by the same cutter Marcello Raffetto bought in 1916. The family members may still be the ones cutting it, as three generations still work at the shop, cooking everything in small batches following the same recipes their ancestors used a century ago. Another aspect that hasn't changed in more than a hundred years: Raffetto's is still a cash-only establishment, but it's well worth stopping by an ATM before you visit. While the store used to offer meat or cheese raviolis exclusively, their menu has evolved to include eighteen varieties, including truffle, chestnut, and pumpkin raviolis. Don't forget to pick up some of their homemade sauces to top your pasta and ravioli selections. **14**

DÉCOUVERTE

Miel des gratte-ciel

JAM SINCE 1975 MAPLE

re·Berries
sachusetts

HORSE

JE

PLUM JAM

WILD AP

"The Best"

SYRUP

FIG

ATO·JAM

UNION SQUARE & CHELSEA

Here we've combined two adjoining neighborhoods: Union Square and Chelsea. Union Square encompasses a large neighborhood beginning at the Flatiron Building on Twenty-Third Street and Broadway and radiating in a large triangle southwest and east to Fourteenth Street, bounded on the west by Sixth Avenue and on the east by Park Avenue.

In the 1930s, Union Square was a nexus of the American labor movement; many unions were headquartered in the office buildings that surround the park. Later, Union Square was home to Andy Warhol's Factory. These days, the Union Square area is a mixed commercial and residential neighborhood housing fashion photographers, filmmakers, Internet companies, ad agencies, and loft-dwelling families, along with terrific outdoor markets.

Chelsea, west of Seventh Avenue, was once a sleepy neighborhood of graceful brownstones, old trees, and small shops. The Episcopal Seminary of New York gives the area the character of a Cambridge college. In the early 2000s, Chelsea was discovered by artists of every generation and their dealers. The neighborhood now extends to the industrial blocks from Fourteenth Street to Thirty-Fourth Street and encompasses a lively mix of edgy galleries, late-night clubs, the High Line, and trendy restaurants.

Bookended by the Union Square Greenmarket to the east and Chelsea Market to the west, these two neighborhoods are brimming with exciting new food stores.

BEDFORD CHEESE SHOP

Do you remember when it was nearly impossible to find artisanal cheeses in the city? Over the past twenty years, there has been a cheese revolution across the United States and especially in New York City, throughout all five boroughs. We first met Charlotte Kamin at the Bedford Cheese Shop's flagship store on Bedford Avenue in Brooklyn. Young and incredibly knowledgeable about cheese, she gladly spent as much time as it took to answer every question we had about her irresistible cheese offerings. Words such as *crumbly, tangy, rich, creamy, gooey,* and *stinky* were bandied about.

She opened a second Bedford Cheese Shop near Union Square, taking her encyclopedic knowledge of cheese (and the shop's local and international selection) with her. Although the carefully curated cheese options are the main draw, refrigerator cases also feature pristine displays of cured meats, olives, pâtés, and prepared foods, and the shelves are lined with mustards, jams, pickles, and crackers, all necessary accompaniments to any good cheese platter. Classes are held at the Manhattan location. 1

BEECHER'S HANDMADE CHEESE

Kurt Beecher Dammeier has been a cheese lover since childhood, and in 2003, he put his passion for cheese into the first Beecher's cheese shop in the heart of Seattle's Pike Place Market. Eight years later, he took his award-winning cheese to New York City, opening Beecher's Handmade Cheese in an eight-thousand-square-foot space in a building with a terra-cotta and brick facade in the Flatiron District.

You can witness firsthand the centuries-old craftsmanship that goes into every batch of cheese, from the milk to the curd to the aging process—just gaze through the big window provided precisely for this purpose. Seven days a week, fresh milk is pumped into the holding tanks at Beecher's kitchens and the cheese-making process begins. Under the skilled watch of the cheese makers, and with a little help from the cows, they create their signature cheeses, the most famous of which is the Marco Polo. The store carries a large assort-ment of cheeses, prepared foods such as macaroni and cheese, charcute-rie, wines, crackers, nuts, sauces, and jams to pair with cheese, as well as a line of outstanding frozen food. **2**

BREADS BAKERY

Master baker Uri Scheft may be new to Manhattan, but his floury status in the international world of bread is already legendary. He made his repu-tation at Tel Aviv's Lehamim Bakery, which he's been running since 2001. In 2013, Scheft partnered with one of his leading fans, New Yorker Gadi Peleg, to open Breads Bakery on Sixteenth Street. Scheft arrived in the United States with all his recipes in hand, and continues to tweak and perfect them with his team of twenty-five. In a short time, Scheft's signature walnut breads, olive loaves, flaky cheese sticks, and chocolate rugelach (inspired by the ones his grandmother made) have garnered him admirers throughout New York.

Born in Israel to Danish parents, Scheft incorporates influences from both countries into the baked goods he sells at Breads Bakery—from the dark rye breads and almond croissants with marzipan inspired by his Scandinavian heritage to Jewish staples like choco-late *babka* and challah. Everything for sale at the shop is made daily in the bakery. In addition to his artisanal, handmade breads, the bakery and café sell sandwiches, mini quiches, cheese straws (the best in town—soft, crisp, and dense with cheese), and pear tarts that are as pleasing to the eyes as they are to the palate. **3**

GOUDA AND CARAWAY SEED ROLLS

Uri Scheft of Breads Bakery

15 ROLLS

FOR THE DOUGH

3 tablespoons compressed fresh
  yeast

4½ cups sifted whole wheat bread
  flour, plus more for flouring work
  surface and bowl

1 large egg

1 tablespoon honey

3 tablespoons unsalted butter, at
  room temperature

1 tablespoon salt

5¼ ounces Gouda cheese, cut into
  ½-inch dice (about 1¼ cups)

2 tablespoons caraway seeds

FOR THE EGG WASH

1 large egg, beaten

PREPARE THE DOUGH (ABOUT 25 MINUTES)

1 Pour 1 cup water into the bowl of a stand mixer and crumble the yeast into it.

Add the flour, egg, honey, butter, and salt. Using the dough hook, knead on low speed for about 4 minutes until combined. Increase the mixer speed to medium and knead for 8 more minutes until a somewhat hard dough is formed.

2 Reduce the mixer speed, add the cheese cubes and caraway seeds, and knead until the cheese and seeds are incorporated into the dough. (Don't worry if the cheese is not completely blended into the dough.)

3 Transfer the dough to a lightly floured work surface. Knead the dough by hand and then roll it into a ball.

PROOF THE DOUGH (ABOUT 90 MINUTES)

1 Place the dough ball in a lightly floured bowl, cover with a clean towel or plastic wrap, and let rise for 50 minutes, or until almost doubled in volume.

2 Using a sharp knife, divide the dough into 15 equal parts. Roll each part into an oval roll shape and arrange them on two baking sheets lined with parchment paper. Brush the rolls with the egg wash.

3 With a small serrated knife, make six diagonal cuts on the top of each roll.

Cover and let them rise for another 30 minutes.

4 When you have about 15 minutes remaining in the proofing process, preheat the oven to 350°F.

BAKE THE ROLLS (ABOUT 15 MINUTES)

Bake the rolls for 15 minutes, or until they are golden brown. Transfer from the baking sheets to a rack and let cool.

CHELSEA MARKET

From the early 1900s to the 1930s, the factories of the National Biscuit Company (a.k.a. Nabisco)—inventors of the Oreo, Mallomar, Nilla Wafer, and Fig Newton—dominated two full blocks between Fifteenth and Sixteenth Streets, from Ninth to Eleventh Avenue. Later, as ovens evolved from vertical to horizontal, Nabisco abandoned its huge city facilities and moved to the suburbs. Land was cheap there, and one-story buildings were more practical for the new ovens. When Chelsea later became fashionable, a developer bought the old Nabisco buildings, renting the upper lofts to artists, photographers, and media companies (the Food Network now occupies one block-size floor). The ground floor was transformed into Chelsea Market, a large corridor with high ceilings, exposed pipes, and displays of factory relics. Food stores, restaurants, a bookstore, a wine store, and even a stand for knife-sharpening (open on the weekends) now populate the place where cookie manufacturing once reigned. Following are some of our frequent stops at Chelsea Market. **4**

Buon Italia

Buon Italia looks like a food warehouse, its wire racks piled high with boxes and huge cans. This is one of the best sources for imported Italian foods. You will find all the standards— imported pasta, San Marzano tomatoes, and wheels of Parmigiano-Reggiano. You'll also find exotic delicacies like *bottarga*, the compressed tuna caviar that we like to shave over simple pastas. Buon Italia carries white truffles in season at very reasonable prices, and, at Christmas, a dozen varieties of panettone, all imported from Italy.

Dickson's Farmstand Meats

The local neighborhood butcher may have gone the way of the horse and cart, but a new wave of butchers is embracing these ethics once again. They want to know where their meat comes from, what the animals are eating, and how they are farmed and harvested. Jake Dickson left the world of marketing to learn from the slaughterhouses, butchers, and livestock coordinators at Stone Barns Center in upstate New York. Now he owns and runs Dickson's. Dickson's also sells poultry, porterhouse beef, rib-eye beef, house-made sausages, charcuterie, and prepared foods. A stop here is a must when you visit Chelsea Market.

4

Doughnuttery

Doughnuts are a distinctly American breakfast pastry with representation in virtually every state, but they command a special place in the lives of busy New Yorkers. Crunchy on the outside and soft inside, the twist here is that the doughnuts are plain, but you can pick from among fifteen unique flavor combinations to dust them in. These include gingerbread/cranberry/sage, lemon/vanilla/poppy seed, or peanut butter/cayenne/pretzel, to name just a few. The doughnuts are made all day and served hot: The machine never stops and neither does the line.

Eleni's New York

What started as a small catering business featuring the oatmeal raisin cookie recipe of the owner's mother has blossomed into an iced-cookie empire, with a shop in Chelsea Market since 1997. For the baker-in-chief, Eleni Gianopulos, who ices all her cookies by hand, icing is an artist's medium. She has thought of every shape and size cookie for every possible occasion, and offers a palette of icing options that would make Renoir proud. If you want to buy treats for a birthday, baby shower, wedding, or office party, or just as a simple thank-you, Eleni's cookies are the way to go.

The Lobster Place

Founded by Rod and Joan MacGregor in 1974, with the goal of bringing the taste of Maine to the Big Apple, this business sells more than a million pounds annually of live lobster, as well as fish, shrimp, shellfish, fish fillets, and whole fish to restaurants and hotels in the New York area. Here, in the company's retail store, you can walk from stand to stand to see what is available, selecting from an alphabet's worth of fresh and prepared fish and seafood, all housed under one roof. Make your selections from the sushi bar, or visit the lobster counter where you can pick a lobster that will be cooked for you on the spot. How

much fresher could it be? The fresh fish department is gigantic, with the offerings displayed beautifully on glistening beds of ice. There are more than twenty different varieties of oysters, lots of clams, sea urchins, and fresh shrimp. More than four decades later, the Lobster Place is still serving some of the best the sea has to offer.

Sarabeth's

Sarabeth and Bill Levine opened their Chelsea Market store to sell the products they've developed at their eponymous New York City restaurants. In the 1980s, Sarabeth Levine started making preserves from her grandmother's recipe. Made in small batches without pectin, these preserves are prized for their hand-cut fruit and distinctive bursts of flavor. Among our favorites are the award-winning blood orange, apricot, pineapple, and chunky apple preserves, as well as the orange apricot and peach apricot marmalades. But don't let Sarabeth's preserves upstage her superb baked goods. The glass cabinets of the Chelsea Market store display rugelach, *palmiers*, and Sarabeth's heart-shaped, chocolate-dipped cookies. Plates are piled high with scones, croissants, and banana-blueberry muffins. And the creamy rice pudding is to die for. If you go early in the morning, you can watch everything being baked behind the big glass window.

Bar Suzette
The Filling Station
The Green
es Torres Chocolate
Lucy's Whey
Kingdom Of Herbs
One Lucky Duck
People's Pops
Tuck Shop
Friedman's Lunch
Buonitalia
attan Fruit Exchange
Sarabeth's Bakery
wery Kitchen Supply
orts from Marrakesh
lsea Market Baskets
Posman Books
L'Arte del Gelato

Anthropologie
Buddakan
Chelsea News
Eleni's New York
Fat Witch Bakery
Chelsea Wine Vault
Ruthy's
Event Space
Amy's Bread
Hale & Hearty Soups
Dickson's Farmstand Mea
Ronnybrook Milk Bar
The Cleaver Co.
The Green Table
Ninth Street Espresso
Nut box
Spices and Tease
Num Pang

ROASTED SALMON

Chelsea Market

SERVES 6

Even if you've never cooked before, you can't go wrong with this recipe. It's incredibly easy, and incredibly good— and not a lot of work for a great weeknight dinner. The secret ingredient here is Jane's Krazy Mixed-Up Salt, a delicious and secret combination that adds a special zip to fish. If you can't find Jane's salt at your grocer, order it online.

> Nonstick cooking spray
> 2 pounds skin-on salmon fillet
> 2 lemons
> ½ cup soy sauce
> ½ cup honey
> ½ cup rice vinegar
> 2 tablespoons Jane's Krazy Mixed-Up Salt
> 6 scallions, finely chopped

1 Preheat the oven to 350°F.

2 Line a baking sheet with aluminum foil and coat with nonstick cooking spray. Place the salmon, skin-side down, on the baking sheet. Squeeze one of the lemons over the salmon.

3 In a small bowl, whisk together the soy sauce, honey, and vinegar and pour the dressing over the fish. Sprinkle with the Jane's Krazy Mixed-Up Salt and the scallions. Close the foil around the salmon by crimping the edges together.

4 Bake for 30 minutes, opening the foil for the last 10 to 15 minutes of baking, until the salmon flakes easily with a fork. Serve on a platter with slices of the remaining lemon.

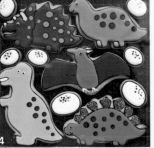

STRAWBERRIES WITH BALSAMIC VINEGAR

Eataly

SERVES 3 TO 4

Choosing an aged balsamic vinegar from Eataly will make this an extra-special treat. The recipe is relatively easy to make, but we're sure you'll be pleasantly surprised to taste how well the combination of pepper and balsamic vinegar develops the aroma of the strawberries. This is especially handy early in the season when strawberries don't have much flavor.

> 4 pounds strawberries
> 1 tablespoon balsamic vinegar
> 1 tablespoon plus 1 teaspoon honey
> Pinch of freshly ground black pepper

1 Clean the strawberries under cold water, cut off the tops, and quarter each one lengthwise. Put the strawberries in a heatproof bowl.

2 In a small saucepan, combine 3 tablespoons water, the balsamic vinegar, and the honey.

Cook over low heat for 5 minutes, stirring with a wooden spoon. The mixture will turn into a syrup. Stir in the pepper.

3 Pour the hot syrup over the strawberries and toss to combine. Cover the bowl with plastic wrap and let the strawberries macerate for 2 hours. Serve at room temperature.

5

EATALY

At the intersection of Fifth Avenue, Broadway, Madison Park, and the Flatiron Building, and a stone's throw to Twenty-Third Street is Eataly, one of the great food emporiums of New York City. This gourmet Italian food market, with partners such as Mario Batali, occupies a five-thousand-square-foot space, as well as a rooftop where tourists, natives, and foodies flock all day long and into the early evening. From the restaurants to the bakery to the pasta bar, Eataly is a people magnet.

The interior is very inviting, with high ceilings, original moldings, columns, and wood flooring. Each section of the market is filled with a specific type of gourmet Italian product, and the quality of the food is extraordinary; this is the place to shop for the very best. Every size and shape of dry pasta and fresh pasta can be found, as well as fresh-baked breads and focaccias that would stop any bread lover in their tracks. Olives, olive oil, vinegar, and sun-dried tomatoes from every region of Italy grace the shelves of one section, while the candy, honey, biscuits, and cakes section joins up with the pastries, which are all made in-house and stand across from the gelato and coffee bars. There is a large butcher counter and abundant fresh fish displays. The charcuterie is a mind-blowing selection of salami, prosciutto, and ham, and the cheese cases are a region-by-region education. Everything you would need to make an outstandingly authentic Italian meal is here, including pots and stylish Italian dinnerware. If you have no idea of what to cook, your first stop should be Eataly's bookstore, where you can buy a cookbook, sip a cappuccino at the espresso bar, pick a recipe, and then start shopping. Inspiration is sure to arrive. **5**

EMPIRE CAKE

Empire Cake is located at Eighth Avenue and Fifteenth Street, where the West Village, Chelsea, and the Meatpacking District meet. The whimsical window displays change with each holiday: lots of Valentines for February 14, turkeys for Thanksgiving, and elaborate cake and cookie themes throughout the year. At Christmas, the window displays rival Bergdorf's. Empire Cake is an ode to nostalgic American baking at its best. The chef gave us an education in her childhood favorites, all of which seem to be baked here. The fluffy coconut Snowball, filled with cream then iced and rolled in shredded coconut, the Ring Ding, that cream-filled chocolate roll dipped in dark chocolate, and then there is the ever-popular black-and-white cookie, which the store sells in three sizes. The list seems endless, and it only gets creamier, sweeter, and more delicious. The cookie selection changes daily but the "Eighth Avenue," made with almond flour, dried fruits, and nuts, is a customer favorite. Others include heart-shaped sugar cookies dipped in dark chocolate, thumbprint cookies, and coconut macaroons. Everything here is a winner—delectable cakes included—and, simply put, it's an empire on the rise. **6**

ITALIAN WINE MERCHANTS

After taking a complete tour of Union Square Greenmarket, you should stop by Italian Wine Merchants on Sixteenth Street on the east side of Union Square. The store holds wine tastings every Saturday, which are open to the public. The facade, appropriately burgundy in color, could be mistaken for that of a warm and cozy restaurant. But, in fact, it is one of the most respected wine stores in the United States, and maybe even the world. Sergio Esposito, the founder of the shop, is so knowledgeable that he could write the history of Italian wines. The Italian Wine Merchants motto is "We bring the world's best wine to our customers." The quality of every bottle—both current releases and vintage wines—is guaranteed by temperature-controlled storage, authenticity, and provenance. Before you visit the store, take a look at the website, which lists more than sixty producers from Italy, as well as a selection from Spain, Argentina, and the United States. **7**

8

8

8

8

9

9

LA BERGAMOTE

In May 1998, executive pastry chef Stephan Willemin and director Romain Lamaze combined their considerable talents to bring La Bergamote to Chelsea. The original pâtisserie, at Ninth Avenue and Twenty-First Street, across the street from the Episcopal Seminary, was a wonderfully peaceful place to stop in the morning for a croissant, coffee, and the *New York Times*. The new location at Ninth and Twentieth, although not directly across from the seminary, is still what you might call a religious experience. La Bergamote has perfected the art of *viennoiserie*, beginning with heavenly croissants, among the best we've had anywhere, and has extended its range to include traditional French pastries like the Concorde, a chocolate lover's dream consisting of a chocolate meringue base, a chocolate mousse filling, and dark chocolate shavings. Try the Bergamotier, the coconut crème brûlée, the Black Forest cake, or one of the three decadent chocolates mousses. **8**

N.Y. CAKE

Whatever you're planning to bake, from a tray of butter cookies to a multitier marzipan wedding cake, start here, at the Home Depot of baking supplies. But don't expect orderly aisles; here the displays stack silicone cookie molds next to pastry bags with interchangeable nozzles, all precariously balanced on columns of Valrhona chocolate. One wall displays edible flowers, food colorants, powdered icing, edible gold leaf, cartoon decals, and a fabulous array of cookie cutters. A serious baker might spend a few days here, browsing the awesome arsenal of baking trays, cake pans, dough cutters, electric mixers, and other plug-in gadgets. Even if you consider yourself baking-averse, this store will arouse an irrepressible urge to preheat your oven, stir some batter, and celebrate a cake-worthy occasion. And if you want to learn how to decorate a cake from start to finish, sign up for some N.Y. Cake Academy classes, which are held in the back of the store. **9**

UNION SQUARE GREENMARKET

The Union Square Greenmarket is the centerpiece of New York City's long-term effort to support local agriculture and bring farm-fresh food to city residents. Smaller markets operate in neighborhoods throughout the five boroughs, but the one at Union Square is the largest. Mondays, Wednesdays, Fridays, and Saturdays—year-round and in every kind of weather—farmers and food artisans from New Jersey, New York, Connecticut, Pennsylvania, and Vermont leave home before dawn and set up their stands on the asphalt walks surrounding the park. Vendors can sell only products they have farmed, produced, caught, or raised themselves, which means you won't find peaches in December, pumpkins in July, or "flash-frozen" Chilean sea bass at any time. This tent city of farm stands sits side by side with the break-dancers, skateboarders, buskers, panhandlers, students, and assorted street characters who congregate in Union Square.

The shopping crowd always seems joyful, and ranges from preschoolers ogling sunflowers to senior citizens negotiating the price of apples. On weekends, the market feels like a purposeful carnival, sellers hawking their wares, customers squeezing tomato after tomato until someone on line shouts, "Hey, it's a tomato, not a car." Union Square is surrounded by a bevy of fine restaurants. Chances are that the hefty fellow next to you rummaging through the garlic ramps is indeed the same cook you've seen on television. Master chefs, accompanied by their assistants, depend on this market for local vegetables, fruits, cheeses, poultry, meats—and inspiration. Chefs arrive first thing in the morning and then again during the day, depending on the menu. Often they let the market decide their specials. At the market, it's best to "ad lib"; leave your shopping list at home and explore. On the following page, we have selected a few of our favorite stands, but you'll also find your own and, in so doing, echo the words of songwriter Ry Cooder: "If you look and see / I know you will agree / That the farmer is the man who feeds us all." **10**

Andrew's Honey

Andrew Cote is a keeper of many bees and a man of many talents, including martial arts. The fourth-generation beekeeper manages about fifty colonies across the city, including at the Waldorf Astoria, which houses 360,000 European honeybees in six hives on its twentieth-floor rooftop. One of New York City's pioneering beekeepers, he has installed more than two hundred hives on rooftops around Manhattan, Brooklyn, Queens, and Westchester County. If he is not on a roof checking his beehives, you have a good chance of meeting him in person at the market, where he sells his rich and creamy honey. In the summer he brings along a hundred bees secured in a transparent tank, which allows customers a firsthand view of how honey is made. Cote's honey is good on just about anything and, as a bonus, his royal jelly and bee pollen may help you fight off a New York cold or summer allergies.

Blue Moon Fish

Blue Moon's catch comes straight off its eponymous boat. Alex and Stephanie Villani fish the waters off eastern Long Island in their steel-hulled trawler and bring the catch straight to Union Square Greenmarket and other venues around New York City. The selection of fresh fish and shellfish is seasonal, but you'll find fluke, sea bass, and skate almost all year round. You won't find fresher fish unless you catch it yourself.

Deep Mountain Maple

Howie and Steph Cantor have been producing maple syrup in Vermont's Northeast Kingdom for more than twenty-five years. There is no activity that ties a person to the whims of nature as much as sugaring, and Deep Mountain maple syrup is bottled on the farm, in their own canning facility. All their fine maple candies and other maple products are made there as well. The Cantors seek to manage the forest in a way that sustains it and their future as sugar makers. They drive 350 miles to the market to bring New York City residents some of the best maple syrup and maple candies the East Coast has to offer.

Martin's Pretzels

These guys never miss a market: Whether it's 10 below or 110 in the shade, Martin's sells crisp, salty, home-baked pretzels. Good thing—there are more and more New Yorkers who cannot get through the day without their Martin's Pretzels; we've seen lines form during a blizzard. Buy a bag and munch your way through the market.

Migliorelli Farm

In 1933 Angelo Migliorelli immigrated to the Bronx from the Lazio region of Italy with only the clothes on his back and a sack of rapini seeds (better known as broccoli rabe). More than eighty years later, the Migliorelli family has parlayed their grandfather's passion for these pungent greens into a thriving produce business with more than six hundred acres under cultivation. To farm those acres, Ken Migliorelli uses a system that greatly reduces the need for dangerous pesticides, and he's secured an agreement with New York state that his land will be farmland forever. All the fruit and vegetables picked on the farm are sold within twenty-four hours, so if you buy produce from the Migliorelli stand, you can be confident of its freshness. The selection varies from season to season, but the options are always so abundant that you can pick up ingredients for a bountiful farm-fresh salad anytime.

APPLE CRISP MIMI STYLE

Union Square Greenmarket

SERVES 6 TO 8

Maddie Fennebresque keeps her grandmother's tradition alive by making this dessert for her entire family every Thanksgiving and Christmas. It took her several tries to decipher her grandmother's handwriting, but now at the age of twenty-one she can share Mimi's secret apple crisp recipe with you.

2 cups sugar
1 cup (2 sticks) unsalted butter, at room temperature, plus more for greasing pan
2 cups all-purpose flour
10 McIntosh apples, cored, peeled, and cut into fine wedges
Pint of vanilla ice cream (optional)

1 Preheat the oven to 350°F. Lightly butter a 9 by 13-inch baking dish.

2 In a large bowl, using your hands, combine the sugar, butter, and flour until the topping mixture is crumbly.

3 Pour the apples into the dish to cover the bottom and scatter the crumbly mixture evenly over the apples.

4 Pop the dish into the oven for 45 minutes, until the topping is golden brown and the apples are bubbling. Serve warm with vanilla ice cream if desired.

PRIME

UPPER EAST SIDE

Generalizations usually don't work when applied to the neigh-borhoods of New York City, and the Upper East Side is added proof. True, the Upper East Side is home to some of the most prestigious apartment buildings, town houses, mansions, private schools, and exclusive clubs in the city, but it's also home to many of the great museums—the Metropolitan Museum of Art, the Guggenheim, the Frick, the Neue Galerie—and to some of the city's best food stores.

While more diverse than some might think—more young single people and married couples with children are moving there—the demographics of the Upper East Side are definitely not downscale. The majority of residents are still well educated and upper middle class.

Artists, musicians, editors, writers, media people, bankers, lawyers, doctors, businesspeople, and three-quarters of the social registry inhabit the Upper East Side—a sophisticated and demanding group for all things, including food. This explains why the array of food stores on the Upper East Side is so dazzling. It is remarkable to find so many best-in-class food shops in such a concentrated area. Upper East Side food stores have honed their skills and their offerings to accommodate their demanding and affluent customers.

In recent years, Fairway and Whole Foods have opened, and the Second Avenue subway is almost complete, all of which has changed—and will continue to change—the way Upper East Siders shop and live.

AGATA & VALENTINA

Agata & Valentina is not the title of a Bellini work: It is the name of an Upper East Side market that celebrates food with operatic flair. Everyone here loves what they're doing, and the attitude is contagious. Louis Balducci, one of the partners, told us that this positive, joyful attitude is no accident, as the shop hires people who will relate well to their customers, and then teaches them the food business. And the food here is as good as the service.

Agata & Valentina makes mozzarella by hand, and if you arrive early enough you can watch it happen. The burrata arrives weekly from Corato, Balducci's hometown in Italy. The rest of the cheese collection is extensive—and quite good. Agata & Valentina makes great fresh pasta, which hangs in uncut sheets on wooden racks from the ceiling. The seafood is excellent, bought fresh every day at the Hunts Point fish market. The pizza oven works all day, turning out thin, crisp-crusted pizza covered with rich San Marzano tomato sauce, buffalo mozzarella, and whatever toppings you might choose. The meat department features prime beef, and on the rotisserie there's excellent roasted chicken; the shop sells more than two hundred a day. You'll also find some delightful desserts in the bakery: We recommend the panna cotta. Balducci and his partner, Joe Musco, have opened a second location in Greenwich Village—a smaller version of the original—but the warmth and taste of Italy definitely inhabits the Upper East Side store. **1**

BABETH'S FEAST

We predict that Babeth's Feast will create a gourmet frozen food revolution on the Upper East Side and probably throughout all of New York City (and maybe even the rest of the country, as the company delivers most anywhere). Elisabeth de Kergorlay founded this business to introduce the U.S. market to delicious heat-and-serve gourmet meals, which may sound like an oxymoron, but in Babeth's Feast's case is actually true. For the first few years she worked on turning her own recipes into irresistible frozen meals, and then moved on to source all the best frozen food available—from meat and poultry to vegetables, sauces, appetizers, and desserts. Then in 2015, Kergorlay was ready: She opened her first retail store, on Third Avenue, with a demo kitchen in the back and giant photography of the frozen food displayed on the walls like an art gallery.

Her freezers of ready-to-go frozen fare are so perfectly organized that you can quickly select a meal for two, four, or fifty without breaking a sweat (and prepare it just as easily). Whether you want breakfast, lunch, dinner, or a midnight snack, this is the place where you can pick up just about anything to eat, and you'll have instant satisfaction without cracking a cookbook. The mini pain aux raisins—soft inside, crusty outside—crab cakes, chicken tarragon, and tomato crumble are all outstanding and will turn an average cook into a four-star chef. If you want to be ready when you feel the urge to do some cooking of your own, stock up on her superb collection of flash-frozen meat, fish, and vegetables—they could not taste fresher. If you think you'll have room for dessert, the gelato and sorbet selection is one of the best in the city. The ice bag pack to keep your purchases cold on the way home is totally fashionable—and keep it handy; you will return many times. (If you prefer not to lug your bags home yourself, order online or at the store and your selections will be delivered right to your front door.) **2**

TUNA TARTARE ON WONTON CRISPS WITH GINGER LIME VINAIGRETTE

Babeth's Feast

SERVES 6 TO 8 AS AN HORS D'OEUVRES

We like to serve these tasty bites as an appetizer.

> 1½ pounds frozen tuna steak
> Grated zest of 2 limes
> Juice of 3 limes
> ¼ cup chopped scallions, white and light green parts only
> 2 teaspoons finely grated fresh ginger
> 2 tablespoons finely chopped fresh cilantro
> ½ cup extra-virgin olive oil
> 25 to 30 wonton wrappers, thawed if frozen
> 1 to 2 cups vegetable oil, for frying
> 1 teaspoon salt, plus more as needed
> Black sesame seeds, for sprinkling

1 Defrost the tuna in the refrigerator overnight. With a sharp chef's knife, cut the tuna into ¼-inch cubes and reserve in the fridge.

2 In a bowl, combine the lime zest and juice, scallions, ginger, and cilantro.

Whisk in the olive oil to create a thick vinaigrette and reserve.

3 Cut each wonton wrapper into a 1-inch square. Heat the vegetable oil in a nonstick skillet over medium heat. Working in batches, fry the wontons until they are browned on both sides, about 2 minutes. Transfer to a paper towel and sprinkle with the salt.

4 To assemble the hors d'oeuvres, toss the cubed tuna in the bowl of vinaigrette until coated; taste and adjust for salt. Place a spoonful of tuna on each wonton crisp and sprinkle black sesame seeds on top. Serve immediately.

CANELÉ BY CÉLINE

Canelé by Céline is one of those great American success stories that seem to abound in the food business. We used to see Céline with a stroller filled with boxes of her *canelés*, delivering them directly to the homes of all the Lycée Français families. But one day chef Jean-Georges Vongerichten sampled her *canelés* and asked where he could buy them. It was the beginning of Céline's success story. After experimenting with a few family recipes, she perfected the art of the *canelé*, and even managed to tweak her sweet recipe to create a line of savory *canelés*. For the uninitiated, a *canelé* is a small French pastry with a tender custard center and a thick caramelized crust.

Céline's tiny store is a gem: The exterior features a bright orange facade and a wooden bench to sit on so you can try one of the *canelés* right on the spot. The interior is filled with old furniture and light fixtures made from antique *canelé* molds—with a baking facility in the back. *Canelés* (our favorites are the vanilla, caramel, chorizo, or truffle) and also financiers (named for their resemblance to the small rectangular gold bars once made near the Paris Stock Exchange) are displayed like pieces of jewelry. **3**

DYLAN'S CANDY BAR

What her father did for the tweed suit, Dylan Lauren is doing for the candy store. She's combined a strong sense of design and the ability to create an alternate reality around everyday products. This is not candyland; it's candy universe. The store is enormous, and every square inch is devoted to, well, candy, much of it oversize. The ground floor is dominated by giant lollipops, ornate candy topiary, and the colors, garish anywhere else, here make delightful eye candy. Giant milk and white chocolate bunnies hop through candy foliage. One whole wall is devoted to chocolate-covered items: raisins, peanuts, cherries, malted milk balls. You'll find cotton candy, Sugar Daddies, Pez, gum balls, licorice, Necco Wafers; candies that look like rings, whistles, bracelets, necklaces; candy canes, gummy bears, gummy worms, gumdrops; as well as an ice-cream counter and cupcake display. The stairs to the lower floor are clear plastic filled with gummy bears, and down those stairs is a Candy Hall of Fame, featuring candy choices of the rich and celebrated. And if your kids aren't spoiled enough by your first visit, you can rent the place out for a birthday party. The decor changes to match the holidays, and it's worth a visit just to see the seasonal changes. This place is pure sugar heaven. **4**

ELI'S MARKET AT THE VINEGAR FACTORY

The Vinegar Factory, which houses Eli's gourmet mega market, was actually a real vinegar factory. People don't go to the Vinegar Factory to buy a quart of milk; this is an all-day, all-in-one food-shopping experience. The market's prepared-foods section allows you to take home many of the items on the café's menu, plus a whole lot more: The roasted green beans are always perfect, as are the egg salad and the Tuscan bread soup. As you wander through the market, you'll find a butcher counter stocked with every choice of meat and fowl, an extensive cheese display, antique barrels full of olive oil, towers of jelly jars—and let's not forget the coffees, teas, nuts, and candy. It's a maze of deliciousness. In the building next door to the Vinegar Factory is Eli's Bread, which turns out all the baked goods sold in Eli Zabars's stores and under the Eli's label all over the country. Eli's Bread has become a contender for the best in New York; our favorites are the raisin pecan loaf and the country loaf. The rugelach is also top-notch, bursting with cinnamon, raisins, and nuts. The heat from the bakery's ovens provides added warmth for the Vinegar Factory's rooftop greenhouses, which grow amazing tomatoes, lettuces, and herbs for the market. Eli Zabar has managed to expand one store into an empire: His Vinegar Factory is on the verge of becoming an ecosystem. **5**

LADY M CONFECTIONS

Take twenty paper-thin crêpes, a bowl of chantilly and vanilla custard, and try to make a perfectly round cake that's only three inches thick. Or go to Lady M, a few steps off Madison Avenue, and buy one of its signature *mille crêpes*: It is light, airy, delicious. This very simple jewel of an Upper East Side bakery makes some of the most beautiful cakes we've seen anywhere. They are all made by hand, and every one is a remarkable combination of baker's craft and chef's sensibility, resulting in precision-perfect sweets presented like gems in a jewelry case. If this image doesn't whet your appetite, no worries: There is the *gâteau fromage*, which the shop refers to as "bliss in a bite," or the banana mille-feuille, a strawberry shortcake like you've never seen it, *gâteau au chocolat* for all you chocolate lovers, or simple éclairs. Shop till you drop and then revive yourself with afternoon tea at Lady M. **6**

GÂTEAU DE CRÊPES

Lady M Confections

SERVES 6

This is your chance to try to re-create one of the most luscious, decadent cakes available in New York City. We'll warn you now: Attempting to match the artistry of Lady M's master bakers is no easy task. The toughest part is the dexterity required to stack one layer evenly on top of the next.

FOR THE BATTER
6 tablespoons unsalted butter
3 cups whole milk
6 large eggs
1½ cups all-purpose flour
7 tablespoons granulated sugar
Pinch salt

FOR THE PASTRY CREAM
2 cups whole milk
1 vanilla bean, halved and scraped
6 large egg yolks
½ cup granulated sugar
⅓ cup cornstarch, sifted
3½ tablespoons unsalted butter

FOR ASSEMBLING THE CAKE
Corn oil
2 cups heavy cream
1 tablespoon granulated sugar, plus more if caramelizing the top
3 tablespoons kirsch
Confectioners' sugar, for dusting

The day before you plan to serve the crêpes, make the batter and the pastry cream.

MAKE THE CRÊPE BATTER

1 In a small saucepan, cook the butter until brown like hazelnuts. Set aside.

2 In another small pan, heat the milk until steaming; remove from the heat and let cool for 10 minutes.

3 With a mixer on a medium-low speed, beat together the eggs, flour, sugar, and salt.
   Slowly add the milk and the browned butter. Pour the batter into a container with a spout, cover, and refrigerate overnight.

MAKE THE PASTRY CREAM

1 In a small saucepan, bring the milk with the vanilla bean pod and seeds to a boil, then remove from the heat and set aside for 10 minutes; remove the vanilla bean pod.

2 Fill a large bowl with ice and set aside a small bowl that can hold the finished pastry cream and be placed in this ice bath.

3 In a heavy-bottomed medium saucepan, whisk together the egg yolks, sugar, and cornstarch. Gradually whisk in the hot milk, then place the pan over high heat and bring to a boil, whisking vigorously for 1 to 2 minutes.

4 Press the pastry cream through a fine-mesh sieve into the small bowl. Set the bowl in the ice bath and stir until the pastry cream reaches 140°F on an instant-read thermometer.

5 Stir in the butter. When completely cool, cover and refrigerate overnight.

ASSEMBLE THE CAKE

1 Bring the batter to room temperature. Place a nonstick or well-seasoned 9-inch crêpe pan over medium heat. Swab the surface with oil, then add about 3 tablespoons of the batter and swirl to cover the surface.

2 Cook until the bottom just begins to brown, about 1 minute, then carefully lift an edge and flip the crêpe with your fingers. Cook on the other side for no longer than 5 seconds.

Flip the crêpe onto a baking sheet lined with parchment paper. Repeat until you have 20 perfect crêpes.

3 Pass the pastry cream through a sieve once more. Whip the heavy cream together with the granulated sugar and kirsch until thick; it won't hold peaks. Fold the whipped cream into the pastry cream.

4 Lay one crêpe on a cake plate. Using an icing spatula, completely cover the crêpe with a thin layer of pastry cream (about ¼ cup). Cover with a second crêpe and repeat to make a stack of 20, with the best-looking crêpe on top. Chill in the refrigerator for at least 2 hours.

5 Let the cake sit at room temperature for 30 minutes before serving. If you have a blowtorch, sprinkle the top crêpe with 2 tablespoons granulated sugar and caramelize with the torch; otherwise, dust with confectioners' sugar. Slice like a cake and serve.

LE MOULIN À CAFÉ

In Manhattan, the Germans have Schaller & Weber, the Italians have Little Italy and the famous Di Palo's, the Japanese have Sunrise Mart, Katagiri, and Tokyo Mart where they can find authentic food from their homelands . . . and the Chinese and Koreans have entire neighborhoods (almost) all to themselves. But the French here in New York had no *épicerie* (French grocery store) until Le Moulin à Café came along. The store, which is also a coffee stop in the morning and a restaurant, offers an excellent selection of croissants (made with the finest butter, which is imported frozen from France and which are met with approval by even the most discerning Francophiles), pain au chocolat, *canelés*, and éclair au chocolat. It's the hangout of choice for the French community living in the city. After dropping off their children at the Lycée Français on East Seventy-Sixth Street, fathers enjoy a coffee together while the mothers buy cookies and French products for their kids. Sometimes the line is very long, but the customers who frequent Le Moulin à Café know one another, so the conversation can be very lively and, of course, in French.

Yann N'Diaye, one of the French co-owners, was nostalgic for France and realized he was especially wistful for many traditional French treats and gourmet products that were difficult (or impossible) to find in the States, so he decided to fill all the shelves in the store with any French food he could import to the United States. These included the BN Chocolate Biscuits from his childhood (smiley-face cookies filled with a thick chocolaty spread), as well as Badoit (lightly salty and fizzy water), Dijon mustard, chestnut paste in a tube to top yogurt or whipped cream, Teissere syrup to mix with water or milk (the French equivalent of a soft drink), Cracottes, Pepito, Granola, Barquettes LU, butter biscuits from Brittany in tin boxes. Come back often, as the products arrive from France every week and you wouldn't want to miss out on your own favorites. **7**

LEONARDS' MARKET

Some stores are good at fish, others are good at meat: Leonards' is very good at both. This family business started life as a fish store in 1910. Later the family bought out a German butcher shop and merged it with the fish store. The result is the best fish store–butcher shop in New York. On one side of the store are the fish, buried in pristine ice, bright-eyed and fresh. The poached shrimp and crab cakes are excellent, and the staff will even cook you a fresh lobster while you wait. Bell & Evans natural poultry arrives at Leonards' market fresh each morning in iced crates, never frozen. The butcher shop at the back of the store sells prime beef, veal, and lamb, dry-aged for weeks in their specially built meat locker to ensure maximum tenderness and flavor, and the staff of expert butchers custom cuts each order. What makes this store special is the execution. Leonards' does everything with remarkable precision and care. **8**

LOBEL'S MEAT

Lobel's is the Fabergé of meat. The best, the biggest, and the most expensive—and they make no bones about it. They've been at the same location since 1930, and five generations have carried the business forward. These butchers really know meat. They buy only the top of the prime, which is scarce and difficult to identify. They dry-age the meat for four to six weeks in a temperature-controlled locker at between 31 and 38 degrees Fahrenheit. The aging process breaks down the connective tissue, which makes the meat tender, and when the meat loses more than 30 percent of its moisture, the result is a more concentrated flavor. The costly aging process and the ensuing weight loss explain, at least in part, why Lobel's pricing is so high.

Lobel's also sells prime veal and lamb, Berkshire pork, and poultry. Cook a cut of Lobel's, and you'll realize that what the butchers have been spouting isn't hype. The meat is sensational, tender, and full of flavor, up there with the best we've ever tasted. The capons are also amazingly flavorful, with a slightly stronger taste than chicken. So ignore the prices, plunk down a chunk of change for a couple of steaks, and for one night turn your kitchen into the best steak house in New York. **9**

LUCY'S WHEY

The original Lucy's Whey, a purveyor of carefully selected artisanal and farmstead cheeses, with a focus on American-made cheese, was squeezed into a former barbershop in an alley off North Main Street in Southampton, New York. It has since moved to New York City's Carnegie Hill, the neighborhood from East Eighty-Sixth to East Ninety-Sixth Streets and Fifth to Lexington Avenue. Catherine Bodziner and Lucy Kazickas, the creators of Lucy's Whey, have personal relationships with cheese makers throughout the country, which guarantees the quality and freshness of their products.

In their Carnegie Hill location, they've expanded their selection to offer some European cheeses, including Camembert, Brie, and Quadrello di Bufala. In addition to the cheeses, Lucy's Whey carries a variety of complementary foods, including fresh bread, jams, marmalades, mustards, and chutneys, all from carefully selected niche brands across the United States and around the world. Try the cured olives, handpicked from a Greek farm, imported by Oupia, a small Brooklyn-based company. Lucy's Whey is also available to cater parties; stop by the café adjacent to the store to taste samples. **10**

11

MAISON KAYSER

In 2012, Louis-Jean Egasse and Lou Ramirez opened Maison Kayser, an artisanal French *boulangerie*, on the Upper East Side—and it took the neighborhood by storm. Maison Kayser is true to traditional French artisanal culture, from the aesthetics of the space—the marble counters and the wooden bread racks—to the baguettes and breads, mixed and baked on-site all day long—and the bakery in the back, supervised by baker Yann LeDoux, as are all the other U.S. locations that followed.

Maison Kayser's bread baking is set apart from other bakeries because it uses only natural sourdough leavening, or *levain*, in liquid form—never any commercial yeast—in all its breads or rolls. The method involves a slower, longer fermentation, or rising, which adds taste and complexity to the bread. All the bread, brioche, croissants, baguettes, pain de mie, and walnut bread are produced in small batches, hand-mixed and baked throughout the day. There are so many superb options that it is hard to choose, so buy as many different breads to try as possible, so you don't feel like you missed out on anything. There are pain de gênes, torsade aux olives, pain d'épi, sesame baguettes, whole wheat baguettes, and, last but certainly not least, a baguette covered in poppy seeds. In addition to the breads—the premier reason to visit this establishment—you'll find croissants, pastries, and an assortment of other traditional baked goods. If you are French, the *chouquettes*—light, round, small choux pastries sprinkled with pearl sugar—will bring back childhood memories. **11**

PRIME BUTCHER BAKER

Joey Allaham came from a family of butchers who opened a few of the best kosher steak houses in Manhattan. It was no a surprise when he opened Prime Butcher Baker, a glatt kosher butcher and market, in February 2012. In fact, several rabbis roam the store full-time to make sure everything is made in accordance with kosher law. Many things are special here: The window to the meat-aging room opens to the street; the market is the first to offer kosher black Angus beef; and the display of sausages and other charcuterie is mouthwatering—goose prosciutto, beef bacon, teriyaki chicken, beef jerky, lamb merguez, duck pâté, and spicy coppa. (And we also love the kebabs: Mediterranean, paprika beef, or lamb.) Everything is fresh, delicious, and beautifully cooked.

When you enter Prime Butcher Baker, everything is about the meat, but as the store's name promises, there is also a bakery in the back; it's famous for its hamantaschen filled with poppy seeds or nuts, orange, and dates (the poppy is our favorite). The frozen-food section is chock-full of soups, an assortment of sliders, potato pancakes, and blintzes, and a whole lot more. No Jewish holiday dinner would be complete without a trip to Prime Butcher Baker. **12**

WHOLE ROASTED CHICKEN WITH ROSEMARY

Courtesy of Prime Butcher Baker from the book *The Prime Grill Cookbook: Redefining the Kosher Experience.*

SERVES 4

FOR THE MARINADE

¾ cup Dijon mustard

2 tablespoons low-sodium soy sauce

1 bunch fresh rosemary, leaves removed from the stem and chopped

FOR THE MIREPOIX

1 large white onion, cut into medium dice

2 stalks celery, cut into medium dice

1 carrot, cut into medium dice

FOR THE ROASTED CHICKEN

1 (3½-pound) whole broiler chicken (wingettes removed)

1 bunch fresh rosemary

1 bunch fresh thyme

2 dried bay leaves, hand crushed

1 head garlic, cut in half

1 lemon, cut in half

2 to 3 tablespoons extra-light olive oil

Salt and freshly ground black pepper

FOR THE GRAVY

2 tablespoons all-purpose flour

2 cups chicken stock, chilled

1 bunch fresh rosemary

Salt and freshly ground black pepper

1 Preheat the oven to 450°F. Combine all the marinade ingredients in a roasting pan and sprinkle the mirepoix in the bottom of the pan.

2 Place the chicken on a clean surface and season the cavity with salt and pepper. Stuff the chicken with the rosemary, thyme, bay leaf, garlic, and lemon. Truss the chicken. With your hand massage the chicken with oil and season with a touch of salt and pepper. Place the whole chicken on top of the mirepoix and marinade. Sear in the oven for 15 minutes. Reduce the oven temperature to 350°F, baste the chicken with the marinade, and return it to the oven. Repeat the process every 10 minutes for approximately 1 hour total, until the juices run clear and the chicken is fully cooked.

3 Remove the chicken from the roasting pan and set aside on a carving board; the mirepoix remains in the pan to create the gravy. Place the roasting pan over medium heat and dust the contents of the pan with the flour. Stir and cook for 2 to 3 minutes, until the flour is browned. Slowly add the cold chicken stock and the whole rosemary sprigs, whisking to remove any lumps. Let simmer for 8 to 10 minutes over low heat. Strain the gravy through a fine sieve, pressing the roasted mirepoix with a spatula or a wooden spoon to extract

additional gravy. Add salt and pepper if needed.

4 Carve the chicken into eight portions and serve with the warm gravy.

SABLE'S SMOKED FISH

Kenny and Danny Sze perfected their smoked fish skills as the managers of the appetizer department at Zabar's before they set off on their own and opened Sable's. The result is excellent smoked salmon, sable, and sturgeon, perfectly cut and trimmed. It's obvious that they didn't waste time or money on interior design or graphics; the store borrows its decorative motif from a high school yearbook: Pictures by the thousands of customers past and present are the wallpaper, and all the signs are handwritten on the same paper that wraps the fish. The focus here is on the fish only. This single-mindedness shows in the quality of the food. Sable's offers excellent lobster salad, smoked lake sturgeon, eastern Gaspé salmon, gravlax salmon with dill, whitefish, smoked mackerel fillet, smoked tuna, smoked Scottish kippers, poached salmon, and more. If you love bagels, cream cheese, and Nova, this is the place for you. **13**

SCHALLER & WEBER

Yorkville runs from Eightieth to Ninetieth Streets east of Lexington Avenue. Many years ago it was called Germantown, home to the largest German community in the city. German restaurants, beer halls, butchers, and delicatessens lined Eighty-Sixth Street from Lexington to the East River. But slowly, as real estate values increased, first- and second-generation German families were displaced by young professionals, and one by one the German stores slowly disappeared.

Today only Schaller & Weber remains. Fortunately it's one of the best sausage makers in the world. Germany is supposed to be the sausage capital of the world, but every year Schaller & Weber enters sausage competitions all over Europe and consistently brings back the bacon. This is no surprise: The knackwurst, bratwurst, liverwurst, and *cervelat* (a German salami) deserve their august reputation. The most popular sausage here is the bockwurst, which is very mild, and made from veal and pork. Other attractions include three kinds of potato salad: German, German with bacon, and American. They're all good, but we especially love the German potato salad. This holdover from old Yorkville is world famous, and deservedly so. **14**

WILLIAM POLL

William Poll is one of the oldest caterers in town. It has been in business for more than ninety years and in the same location on Lexington Avenue for more than sixty years. If you haven't visited, it is a must. Stanley, the founder's nephew, will greet you with a smile as you enter and tell you entertaining stories about William Poll. Everything is made fresh, from the original traditional recipes, every day in the open kitchen in the back of the store.

The tried-and-true dishes include deviled eggs, potpie, lobster dip, and baked potatoes, which are legendary. Customers know William Poll's products so well they need not even come into the store. Orders are phoned in starting in the early morning and wait at the front door for delivery. But for us the real joy is a visit to the store; it's a step back in time. We look forward to Stanley's coming down the stairs to tell us about how the food is made, how the neighborhood has changed, his loyal customers, and his wife, a gorgeous blond who ran the business with him for decades—it's an experience that can last for hours. If you do not have time, just talk directly to the cooks working in the kitchen: They know their products inside and out and will give you advice on what to purchase. **16**

SHERRY-LEHMANN

Sherry-Lehmann is a cross between a wine shop and an investment bank. It is one of New York's oldest and best wine shops. Back when businesspeople were wading through three-martini lunches, Sherry-Lehmann was one of the first stores to take wine seriously, and the foresight has paid off. The selection is vast and well chosen; the Bordeaux and Burgundy sections are encyclopedic. A big business here is wine futures, the buying and selling of vintages and speculation before they come out, in the hopes that once on the market their values will increase. Here's a shopping tip: The next time your significant other gets impatient as you peruse the racks at Barneys, send him one block away to Sherry-Lehmann, where there's a good chance he'll spend more than you. **15**

UPPER WEST SIDE

The Upper West Side is easily the lushest neighborhood in New York, bounded on the east by Central Park and on the west by the wide swath of Riverside Park and the Hudson River. It's bordered on the south by Fifty-Ninth Street and on the north by 125th Street, and encompasses the hilly beauty of Morningside Park.

The apartment buildings along Central Park West and Riverside Drive are exquisite examples of prewar residential architecture. The side streets are lined with beautifully preserved four- and five-story town houses, and everywhere you look you'll find great food stores, from the tiniest bodega to sprawling supermarkets.

Although the Upper West Side shares Central Park with the Upper East Side, that and the weather about cover what the two neighborhoods have in common. Even if some long-term West Siders complain that their neighborhood has become too gentrified, the mix here is still eclectic. The West Side is intellectual and artistic, gritty and colorful, European and Latin, down to earth, in touch with its ethnic roots.

Despite the Columbus Circle malls and the blooming of fancy new hotels, the area from Columbus Circle to Columbia University is more diverse racially, religiously, and economically than its neighbor on the other side of the park. The food stores reflect this diversity. On the Upper West Side, hundred-year-old appetizing stores stand comfortably next to trendy bakeries. Each new generation has left its stamp on the community. The result is that while individuals may move on, the food stores they've created often continue to flourish.

ABSOLUTE BAGELS

In an era when any piece of dough with a hole poked through it can be called a bagel, Absolute Bagels makes the authentic item—made from high-gluten flour, yeast, and malt, hand-rolled, then boiled and baked. The result is perfection: crunchy outside, chewy inside, with a distinctive woody taste. The master behind this Olympian bagel is Sam Thonkrieng, who was born in Thailand. Thonkrieng worked in several bagel bakeries and later bought Absolute Bagels from the original owner. He saw the short-cuts that other bagel makers were taking and resolved to do things right. Absolute Bagel is the Greenwich clock of bagels, the standard for all others. **1**

BARNEY GREENGRASS

The Upper West Side absorbed three waves of Jewish immigration: at the turn of the twentieth century, and before and after World War II. One effect of this triple influx on the neighborhood is the highest concentration of smoked fish vendors in the world. Though very different in ambience, the two best sources—Barney Greengrass and Murray's Sturgeon (see page 132)—are located within blocks of each other in the West Eighties. Barney Greengrass has been at the same location since 1908: The roster of devoted customers is a Who's Who of New York. The original owner, Barney Greengrass, a.k.a. the Sturgeon King, was featured in so many travel books that you can still hear tourists from all over the world mouth his mantra: "Lox 'n' eggs." Gary Greengrass, his grandson, is just as passionate about the business and the quality of the food. As you enter Barney Greengrass, the long counter on the right is your destination for world-class sturgeon and chopped liver. To your left is the restaurant, furnished with green Formica tables and aluminum chairs that look like they've been lifted from a 1950s sitcom. Aside from the smoked fish and chopped liver, our other favorites are the borscht, great with a spoonful of sour cream, and the kugel (noodle pudding). Anybody who goes to New York should make a pilgrimage to this legendary spot, meet Gary Greengrass, and sit down for "a nice piece of fish." **2**

G-FREE NYC

For those of you who can't eat gluten for health reasons (or just feel better when you avoid it), this is the one-stop shop for you. If you fit that profile, then you've likely tasted too many gluten-free products that resemble cardboard. But at G-Free, all the products have been taste tested, taking the guesswork out of your shopping; G-Free carries only those items that have great flavor and a texture appropriate to the gluten-containing originals.

G-Free is small but cozy and yet it manages to carry just about anything you could want to create a satisfying gluten-free meal. Skeptics, your mind and your palate will be changed after you visit this shop. The owner is very informative and will help you choose the right foods for your dietary needs (see also G-Free's website for links to a ton of information about celiac disease and gluten intolerance, plus restaurant and recipe resources). She also had the insight to track down a group of talented bakers who deliver fresh baked goods to the store directly. Do not miss the frozen grain bread or the fresh cookies, which are so good, you could devour half a dozen on the bench in front of the store. And, the best news is, if you can't make the trip, G-Free delivers. **3**

GASTRONOMIE 491

Nicole Ahronee grew up amid the lively food markets of Rome and southern France. After attending Wellesley College and Columbia University, Ahronee turned to the world of gemology. Since food was central to her Mediterranean upbringing, she made a career move: the next step was creating Gastronomie 491, an Upper West Side specialty food market and café. Ahronee's goal for her store was to provide the neighborhood with great fresh food. The day we visited, big platters of sautéed kale, steamed broccolini, ratatouille, roasted vegetables, grilled asparagus, roasted new potatoes, and an assortment of salads were all on offer. We wanted to taste everything—and so will you. In addition to the prepared foods, browse through the aisles, where you'll find enough tempting ingredients to inspire a dinner for two or twenty. The well-curated shelves are filled with sauces, condiments, spices, pastas, jams, teas, and more. And to help complete your meals, you'll find seasonal fresh fruits and vegetables and a freezer full of ice cream and sorbet. The cheese and charcuterie counter is well stocked and a favorite in the neighborhood. Don't pass up the beers, selected from fifty small breweries. Walk in, enjoy a cappuccino and a very decadent pastry or macaron, then do your grocery shopping for the day. Gastronomie 491 is a unique Upper West Side shopping experience, and if you wish, find Ahronee and she will happily walk you through this gem. **4**

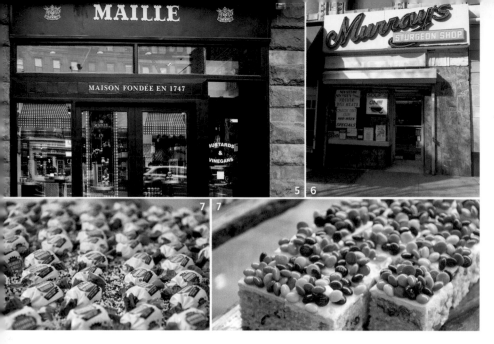

TREAT HOUSE

In October 2011, Daniel and Eli Russell were charged with raising fifty dollars apiece for charity and looked to their parents, Chris and Jennifer, for help. The resulting bake sale, which featured old-fashioned crispy rice treats, marshmallowed into a magical dream. After selling their first batch of treats and watching a line of people return for more, the lightbulbs went off. The family contacted pastry chef Wendy Israel, who helped them create a line of flavors that would appeal not only to children but to grown-ups, too. The Russells were on their way to opening a business based on the simple idea of mixing marshmallows with crispy rice cereal and adding whimsical flavors and toppings.

Treat House offers fun, flavorful twists on the favorite childhood treat. The treats may be topped with M&M's, wrapped bubble gum, big red lips, gummy bears, chocolate footballs, and, last but certainly not least, chocolate laced with chile. All are certified kosher dairy, and unless specified otherwise, they are also gluten-free, dairy-free, and nut-free. The Treat House's homemade marshmallows are made using raw cane sugar, never corn syrup. The shop also sells wholesome breakfast bars, which contain brown rice, oats, flax, dried fruits, and seeds (some contain nuts). **7**

MAILLE

This store is a celebration of the Maille dynasty, which Antoine-Claude Maille began in 1720. The shop offers thirty-four unique mustard flavors, nine vinegars, cornichons, oils, and much more. In addition to the classic Dijon and whole-grain flavors are exotic alternatives such as fig, coriander, and white wine; morel mushroom and Chablis; and apricot, curry spices, and white wine. Maille mustards are unique, strong, and dense with flavor. All the offerings are displayed in a myriad of small transparent pots; tasting is encouraged. Maille mustards and vinegars are staples in any French fridge, and one of the secret ingredients for thickening a sauce, or brightening up a salad dressing or a sandwich. **5**

MURRAY'S STURGEON SHOP

Murray's Sturgeon has been selling smoked salmon, sturgeon, whitefish, chubs, kippered salmon, and a great selection of flavored cream cheeses for more than sixty years. This is a spare, no-nonsense store with efficient, helpful service. It's reassuring to know that, anywhere you go on the Upper West Side, you are within close reach of a quarter pound of smoked salmon. For all you tuna salad aficionados, the best one can be found here. Go also for the herring salad, the spinach and egg salad, and don't forget the kosher meats. Murray's exudes Old-World charm with some of the best smoked fish and delicacies to go with it. **6**

ZABAR'S

Which came first? Zabar's or the Upper West Side? Zabar's opened in 1934, but for many New Yorkers and tourists, their first discovery of the special West Side zeitgeist started with a trip to Zabar's. It is more than a store: It's a life experience. The first time you go there, you may be overwhelmed by the rush and noise of the crowd and by the overflowing displays. Breathe deeply and center yourself. Soon the wonders of Zabar's will come into focus.

First, the smoked fish counter. Take a ticket and wait for the counterman to call your number. Meanwhile, survey the fish inside the glass case—eastern Nova, western Nova, Scottish salmon, whitefish, chubs, sturgeon, and several types of pickled herring. No matter how many people are waiting, the countermen will give you a couple of tastes. Some countermen will flirt or joke (in English, Yiddish, or Korean); other countermen are silent, their attention on their long, thin knives and the fish fillet before them. Next, follow your nose to the coffee section. Zabar's roasts and grinds its own. You can choose whole beans or have the coffee ground to your specifications. The Colombian Supreme, Kenya AA, and double Dark Espresso are our favorites. Still on the first floor, head for the ample cheese selection, the bakery, the prepared foods counter, and the butcher. If kitchen equipment and housewares are of interest, climb the stairs to the second floor. The selection is awe-inspiring. We counted a dozen different espresso machines. Even if your cooking is limited to the microwave, you'll find some enchanting gadget or machine. **8**

BRONX

The area around Arthur Avenue in the Bronx is Little Italy North, and it shares much of the same history as its older sibling to the south. Italian immigrants settled this area in the early twentieth century, creating an enclave of Italian grocers, salumerias, cheese stores, and restaurants, all centered around Our Lady of Mount Carmel Church. Over the years, as the immigrant families prospered and migrated to greener suburbs, they were replaced by Albanians, Mexicans, and Russians. But while Manhattan's Little Italy is today more a memory than a reality, having been largely swallowed up by an ever-expanding Chinatown, the stores of Arthur Avenue remain stalwartly Italian, run by the second and third generations of the families who founded them. Italian families from all over the region return to Arthur Avenue and their roots—at least for an afternoon of shopping and good food. After all, it's hard to find really good *mesamanich* sausage in Darien, Connecticut.

These returnees and the new immigrant communities have kept the stores of Arthur Avenue thriving. They've also been discovered by the food cognoscenti, so that on a weekday morning you just might spot a few world-famous chefs poking around the shops searching out the best ingredients for their next brilliant pasta dish.

Mount Carmel is the best place to start your exploration, and as you wander down Arthur Avenue you will be delighted by the quality of the food and the exuberance of the people.

ADDEO & SONS BAKERY

At Hughes Avenue and East 186th Street, you will notice the giant Addeo & Sons sign rather than the store-front, but, yes, there is a shop under the giant banner. This old-fashioned, family-owned Italian bakery offers a limited selection, but every item is delicious. At Addeo, the bread is crispy outside and really moist inside. You will come back again and again after you have tried the breadsticks and the fresh pizza dough. **1**

ARTHUR AVENUE RETAIL MARKET

More than half a century before Eataly opened, the Bronx had its own indoor Italian market—Arthur Avenue Retail Market—where an assortment of small businesses has long thrived under one skylit roof. The market was built by Mayor La Guardia in 1940 to house the pushcart vendors who were the life-blood of this community, and you can still feel the pushcart spirit throughout the structure. Several years ago, the owners of the small businesses housed there joined together to buy the market from the city and form a cooperative. The market members chose their president from among the vendors, and its management is a miracle of capitalist collectivism. Most of the vendors sell food items (though a cigar maker and a florist have shops near the entrance), and each store has its own specialty. All the vendors are very friendly and always eager to share their version of the market's history and their own. **2**

Mike's Deli & Arthur Avenue Caterers

A "World Famous Deli" that actu-ally is world famous. Every inch of the ceiling and the walls is cov-ered with cheeses and dried sau-sage. There is so much food here that it would be hard to see the people behind the counter if they weren't larger than life. The deli is run by Mike Greco and his son David. Greco was the subject of a one-man show written by one of his sons called *Behind the Counter with Mussolini*, which might tell you a lot about Greco's manage-ment style, but doesn't reflect his charm and willingness to help. (He'll also give you a taste of just about anything you ask for.) Ham, sausage, prosciutto, and cheese are the specialties here, and once you've sampled them at the store you can order from the very complete website. The sandwiches here are also larger than life, overflowing with combinations of Asiago, provolone, Parmesan, sausage, prosciutto, ham, peppers, and olives. Take your feast and have a seat at the café next door.

Mount Carmel Gourmet Food Shop

This shop specializes in artisanal pastas—pappardelle, spaghetti, orec-chiette, and bucatini—along with fine olive oil and balsamic vinegar. The olive oil is from Gianfranco Becchina, an Italian maker who produces exquisite, unfiltered, chemical-free oils. There is a feeling here of a time capsule pre-serving the best of the Old World.

Peter's Meat Market

This is organ meat central. You'll find every type of tripe (pork, beef, lamb), sweetbreads, kidneys, and veal heads, all of the finest quality—and the butchers cannot wait to explain everything in the cases. The shop also sells more popular parts of the animal, ready to be cooked. The veal rollatini and beef and pork braciole are both first rate.

BIANCARDI MEATS

This is an authentic butcher shop; lamb and unskinned rabbits hang in the windows. The meat here is excellent, as is the service. The guys behind the counter seem to know all their customers' names, and the lines, particularly around holidays, can snake around the store. Biancardi has been operated by the same family since 1932. It's a great place to experience the atmosphere of an Italian village butcher shop. The house is known for its stuffed pork chops and house-cured pancetta. **3**

BORGATTI'S RAVIOLI & EGG NOODLES

Down the block from the market and facing the church is a store with a window full of American flags, a statue of the Virgin Mary, and very little evidence that it has been one of the best ravioli stores in New York since 1935. Inside, every inch of space is occupied by religious images, family pictures, and drying pasta. Spaghetti hangs from the ceiling and trays of ravioli are everywhere.

Imagine a pasta factory on a small boat. To perform any task, something must be moved. The pasta machines, all vintage models, are stowed in the back of the store and rolled out one at a time for each step of the process. The proprietor, Mario Borgatti, took over his parents' business twenty years ago and never left. All the staff are long-timers: One of the pasta makers we met has been working in the store for more than twenty years. The experience shows in the quality of the beautifully made pasta and ravioli and definitely in the taste. The texture is perfect, and the ravioli fillings are amazingly light and flavorful. These hardworking craftspeople turn out a superb product, a must-try. And, of course, they are closed on Sunday and Monday. **4**

BOLOGNESE-STYLE MEAT SAUCE
Borgatti's Ravioli & Egg Noodles

SERVES 4 TO 6

The Borgatti grandparents brought family recipes from Bologna to the United States, and a few generations later the family is still making the same recipes at the store. Serve with Borgatti's fresh pasta.

  2 ounces salt pork, diced
  ⅓ cup olive oil
  1 clove garlic, finely chopped
  ½ cup chopped onion
  1 cup chopped carrot
  1 cup chopped celery
  1 pound lean ground beef
  ½ cup white wine
  ½ cup light cream
  1 tablespoon tomato paste
  2 cups chicken broth
  1 cup fresh or frozen peas
  2 tablespoons unsalted butter
  1 teaspoon ground nutmeg
  Salt and freshly ground black
    pepper

1 In a saucepan, heat the salt pork in the oil until it turns light brown. Remove the salt pork from the pan and set aside.

2 In the same pan, brown the garlic to your taste, then add the onion and cook until translucent, stirring

4

frequently. Add the carrot and celery and cook until they soften and start to change color. Add the ground beef, stir to break it up, and cook until it turns brown in color.

3 Pour the wine into the pan and increase the heat to high and bring to a boil; add the light cream and boil for 3 minutes, then reduce the heat.

4 Dilute the tomato paste in the broth and add to the saucepan. Add the peas to the pan, cover, and simmer for 45 minutes.

5 Add the butter and nutmeg and season the sauce with salt and pepper. Stir well and simmer for an additional 45 minutes before serving.

CALABRIA PORK STORE

Following in the family tradition of artisanal sausage making, Nick and Peter took over their parents' business, one of the most unique stores on Arthur Avenue. The outside of Calabria Pork Store looks like any salumeria, but upon entering you might feel as if you've walked into a sausage cave, complete with salamis and dried sausages for stalactites. The sausages, hanging from custom-made wooden racks to dry, take up every available inch of ceiling space. Throughout the year whole pigs are delivered to the shop and transformed into soppressata, pancetta, and several kinds of sausage according to traditional family recipes. The quality of these sausages is unparalleled, and for any sausage lover, a visit is a must. **5**

CALANDRA CHEESE

Depending on where you begin on Arthur Avenue, this family-staffed cheese shop is either the first or the last stop, and a great way to start or finish your trip. The petite storefront is easy to spot because of all the scamorza cheese (some in the shape of little pigs) hanging from racks, like Christmas decorations on a tree. Calandra may be tiny, but it packs in a bounty of irresistibly fresh burrata, burrini, mozzarella, and fresh ricotta. Sal Calandra's mozzarella and ricotta have been named the best in New York many times over. The mozzarella is the freshest you can buy, lightly smoked and available salted or unsalted. And the whole-milk ricotta, sold by the pound, is fresh: You can refrigerate it for five days or buy extra and freeze it, assuming you don't finish it on the ride home. Use the ricotta for pizza, or smear it on a great piece of bread and top with honey, a few nuts, and dried apricots. Be sure to read the board outside that lists all the daily specials: It will surely whet your appetite. **6**

MADONIA BROTHERS BAKERY

The key feature here is the great bread, made by hand and baked in wood-burning ovens. The windows and shelves brim with freshly baked bread—prosciutto bread, provolone bread, cranberry and walnut bread, and *pane di casa*. In keeping with the changing demographics of the neighborhood, this Italian-owned bakery is staffed by Albanian women in starched white aprons, and the service is excellent. To help you decide which of its breads you like best, Madonia Brothers leaves out a tray of samples for its customers. **7**

RANDAZZO'S SEAFOOD

Some of New York's best Italian chefs buy their seafood at Randazzo's, and a walk through the store conjures up delightful visions of *zuppa de pesce*, branzino in parchment, and *linguine alla vongole*. The cases overflow with octopus, clams, scallops, *baccalà*, and a great collection of whole fish. The seafood here is as fresh as you'll find, and the staff is friendly and willing to help you make the best choice of fish or seafood for whatever you decide to cook. The selection at Randazzo's just might inspire you to try your hand at making some *zuppa de pesce* or cioppino of your own. **8**

S&S CHEESECAKE

Even cheesecake snobs know that behind the doors of the unassuming, nondescript building of S&S Cheesecake, they will find the best cheesecake imaginable. S&S Cheesecake established its reputation for excellence more than sixty years ago. You can pick up your cheesecake at the factory or order it online; our favorite flavors are New York style and strawberry. The cheesecakes are also available around New York City, but if you buy them elsewhere, you won't get the chance to meet S&S's extremely charming owner, Yair Ben-Zaken. Each cheesecake sits inside a ring, and the secret to its light and airy texture is that it is baked twice, ensuring that it retains its moistness and rises to perfection. The recipe has not changed since the company's founding, and S&S does not compromise on the quality of the cream cheese, eggs, sugar, and vanilla or other ingredients. S&S has figured out the right method to consistently make a superb cheesecake. **9**

TEITEL BROTHERS

One hundred years after this Italian specialty food shop opened, it still packs in loyal customers, wholesalers, and the general public. Don't be confused by the Star of David on the floor of the entrance: The merchandise is Italian through and through. The star was cemented in place when Austrian immigrants Jacob and Morris Teitel opened the business in 1915. Today, Gilbert Teitel and his sons Jean, Michael, and Eddie stand shoulder to shoulder in white aprons from opening to closing, slicing cheese and salami and calling out "Whose next?" to their customers. Here you can find fifty-gallon tins of extra-virgin cold-pressed Italian olive oil, fifty-pound sacks of flour, and tomato puree by the pound—enough to make pasta for the entire neighborhood. **10**

BROOKLYN

Brooklyn was an independent city until it merged with New York in 1898. If it were still autonomous, Brooklyn would be the fourth-largest city in the United States with almost 2.6 million people. Much of the character outsiders attribute to New York City—the accent, the attitude, and the sense of humor—was born in Brooklyn.

Brooklyn has been called the City of Trees and the City of Churches; we'll go with the City of Food Stores. The diversity and quality of Brooklyn's food shops is without equal, especially in the past decade, with rooftop farms, organic markets, food trucks, Smorgasburg, the Whole Foods Market greenhouse in Greenpoint, and Down to Earth markets, just to name a few. Brooklyn has become an incubator for the food community and a foodie's heaven. It is also a borough of distinct neighborhoods, each with its own character and demographic. Many of the neighborhoods, like Prospect-Lefferts Gardens, Red Hook, and Bushwick, have gentrified at such breakneck speeds that it's hard to keep track of the changes. Others, like Bensonhurst and Bay Ridge, seem untouched by time. In others, like Brooklyn Heights and Park Slope, new residents have slowly changed the character of the neighborhoods, keeping the best of the old while adding new flavor to the mix.

Brooklyn has hundreds of wonderful food stores. The ones listed here are some of the best, but we are sure that as this book goes to press, many more creative and delicious culinary experiences are about to take Brooklyn by storm. While Brooklyn is definitely a part of greater New York City, it is the borough that has most retained its sense of independence, which is fitting for New York City's second city.

BEDFORD-STUYVESANT
DOUGH

Christian Djomatin moved to Brooklyn from Benin, West Africa, and opened Dough in Bed-Stuy in 2010. While the name may leave something to the imagination, upon entering, the comforting smells of baked goods draws you in. The windows are large; there are distressed wooden floors and old-time bakery cases. You can watch the bakers at work as they move to the rhythm of the background music. Rave reviews of Dough's doughnuts abound, even for the simple glazed ones, which have been likened to a religious experience—but tasting is believing. The café au lait and lemon poppy doughnuts are both a revelation, and the blood orange doughnut is tangy and delicious. If you are a traditionalist, you will find the glazed doughnuts very satisfying; the more curious should try the passion fruit doughnut, with its tart-sweet yellow icing. Other inventive flavors include dulce de leche, hibiscus, chocolate cream, lemon meringue, and many more. Consuming these light, puffy, fresh doughnuts is always a joyful experience. While there are only a few stools in the store, you will no doubt walk away with several doughnuts in a brown bag. No use trying to save them: Temptation will win and the bag will be empty by the time you arrive at home. This small but very inviting shop is truly a doughnut lover's dream. **1**

BOERUM HILL
BIEN CUIT

Bien Cuit opened in the Boerum Hill section of Brooklyn in 2011 to rave reviews. Master baker Zachary Golper and his wife and business partner, Kate Wheatcroft, are passionate about the quality of the breads, pastries, tarts, and sandwiches they sell at their French bakery, Bien Cuit, and this fervor is evident the minute you walk through the door. Begin your day with any of the breakfast pastries, and you've set the stage for a good day. Choose from beautifully buttery and flaky plain, chocolate, or almond croissants, or if you prefer savory items, try the ham and Brie or artichoke and goat cheese versions. And no French bakery would be complete without pain aux raisin; Bien Cuit's version features brioche dough, rum-poached black currants, and vanilla pastry cream. Do not miss the miche (a very large rustic sourdough bread), which boasts an extremely crunchy brown crust with a white, airy, delicate crumb. Golper is a true artisan and his love of what he does is in every bite. **2**

NUNU CHOCOLATES

South African chocolatier Justine Pringle first started selling her candies at the concerts of her husband, singer-songwriter Andy Laird. Her chocolates developed such a cult following that she branched out to many Brooklyn food haunts, and, in 2009, opened her first storefront in Brooklyn. After we began spotting Nunu's unmistakable brown boxes with a blue logo in many specialty food stores, we decided to go to the source, where we were lucky enough to watch the caramel being made. The cocoa used to make Nunu's chocolates is a single-origin cocoa bean from a Trintario and Criollo hybrid, grown at a sustainable family-run farm in Santander, Colombia, and the other ingredients are all organic. We recommend that you try the Booze Box, Ganache, and Caramel Blend assortment—you'll find yourself running back to Nunu for more. Making caramel is a tricky task. Nunu's simple recipe begins with water, sugar, and butter; the more elaborate versions can include chocolate, coffee, crème fraîche, and vanilla, as well as nuts and fruits—the quality and balance of the ingredients and the cooking time make all the difference. Nunu, which is famous for its creamy salted caramels (including a chocolate-dipped rendition), has mastered the technique. Be prepared to exercise a little restraint: It is very hard to stop at just one. And don't miss out on a cup of the hot chocolate, reputed to be one of the best in New York. **3**

BOROUGH PARK
HUNGARIAN KOSHER CUISINE

For many American Jews, kugel is the dish that makes them nostalgic for their childhoods. They want exactly the kind of kugel their mothers made, whether it is served weekly at Sabbath or only on the holidays. Shmela Friedman, a soft-spoken father of ten, is the King of Kugel at Hungarian Kosher Cuisine. Kugel is Jewish potato pudding, made here from potatoes, oil, eggs, and salt. No onions, no pepper. The recipe sounds plain, but the difference between a light and delicious kugel and a leaden doorstop is in the hands of the kugel maker. Friedman's kugel is always perfect, whether you go for the sweet or savory varieties—apple, cherry, blueberry, strawberry, or spinach, broccoli, mushroom—all of them served in simple foil trays. The kugel here sells out as fast as it's brought out from the kitchen. Try the potato pancakes with applesauce, too; they will keep you coming back for more. **4**

KORN'S BAKERY

Manhattan has the Garment District, the Fur District, the Meatpacking District, and the Flower District. In Brooklyn we discovered the challah district, on Eighteenth Avenue in Borough Park . . . and Korn's is *the* place for challah bread. Korn's challah is as much a pleasure to look at as it is to eat—check out the skillfulness of the braiding and the way the golden loaves practically glow on the table! For celebrating everything from Hanukkah to Sunday supper, Korn's challah is the right bread for the job. Cut yourself a slice and cherish the pillow-soft interior, simultaneously rich and slightly sweet. Visit this bakery during holidays and you will be dazzled by the racks and racks of these beautiful loaves in every shape and size—some plain, some with raisins, some with sesame seeds, and all delicious. Korn's challah is a religious experience for every faith. **5**

BROOKLYN HEIGHTS
DAMASCUS BREAD & PASTRY SHOP

Brooklyn Heights was once Brooklyn Village, then, during the Revolutionary War, Brooklyn Town, and its cobbled streets still retain their colonial charm. But near the eighteenth-century landmark is Atlantic Avenue, home to the largest collection of Arab-American food stores in the United States. Hassan Halaby opened a Syrian bread bakery in 1930, and his descendants are still here today, baking pita with a passion. The bakery is small but the selection, displayed in a long, blue-paneled glass display case, is grand, offering brick-oven baked pitas, vegetable and meat pies, baklava, bird's nests, kanafa rolls (shredded wheat pastries filled with custard or nut paste), and dozens of other breads and sweets. The craftsmanship of the Halaby family makes it obvious why Damascus has thrived all these years, and why the store is seldom empty. Among the big draws are a crisp, honey-soaked pistachio baklava; rich, fresh-baked, potato-spinach pie; and the fried, almond-filled burma pastry. In addition to all the Middle Eastern pastries, you'll find a wall of refrigerators filled with taramasalata, cucumber salad, yogurt salad, string cheese, halloumi cheese, and feta cheese. At the back of the store, you'll find shelves bursting with spices from every corner of the Middle East. Don't leave without purchasing a hot spinach and cheese pie—you'll want to eat it posthaste. **6**

SAHADI'S

Sahadi's is an authentic Lebanese grocery that's been in business since the turn of the twentieth century; the Atlantic Avenue store opened in 1948. Open sacks of coffee, chickpeas, lentils, black beans, basmati rice, brown rice, white rice, cashews, almonds, walnuts, pecans, peanuts, and myriad spices line the store. The scent in the air changes with every step taken. Sahadi's will sell any of these grains, nuts, and spices by the quarter pound or hundredweight. There are more than a hundred varieties of cheese, including five types of feta and a few cheeses from Lebanon we've never encountered before. Sahadi's carries a large variety of packaged Middle Eastern jams, pickles, syrups, and sauces under the Al Wadi brand. The prepared foods are excellent: The hummus and baba ghanoush are among the best we've ever tried. A few hours browsing at Sahadi's is an immersion course in Middle Eastern food. **7**

BRIGHTON BEACH
BRIGHTON BAZAAR

Brighton Beach, a.k.a. Little Odessa, is home to the largest and most prosperous Russian and Ukrainian populations this side of the Atlantic. Since M&I Foods, the mecca of grocers in Brighton Beach, closed, Brighton Bazaar is the best choice. This giant corner supermarket manages to import just about every available Russian product; the food selection would be greeted warmly in Moscow or Kiev. There is an endless variety of hot foods, an enormous pickle bar (pickled watermelon appears regularly), a crêpe bar, a prepared food section, fresh bread and baked goods for every occasion, and so much more. For obvious reasons we got stuck in the pastry department filled with halva, pierogi, and poppy seed cakes, but managed to make our way to the butcher and meat department as well as the fresh and smoked fish section. It might be prudent to take somebody with you who speaks Russian, but if that's not possible there will be a vendor or a customer to help you navigate your way through the store. This is a Russian *prazdnik* at its best. **8**

COBBLE HILL
FISH TALES

Unlike Brooklyn Heights, its neighbor to the north, Cobble Hill has managed to keep its neighborhood feel almost intact. This Cobble Hill seafood store is as briny and fresh as an ocean breeze. The fish, displayed on a blanket of ice on a sleek refrigerated table, speak for themselves: Their eyes are bright and clear, and their skin color is vivid, both signs of fresh fish. All the fish are labeled, not only with their names, but also with where they were caught, their nutritional value, and how they should be prepared. The store also sells sushi-grade fish. To be eaten raw, the fish must be flash-frozen for fifteen hours at 15 degrees Fahrenheit; if you're of a mind to make your own sushi, this is the place to buy the raw material. **10**

BUSHWICK
TORTILLERIA MEXICANA LOS HERMANOS

If not for the aroma of toasting corn wafting from its nondescript storefront you might walk right past Los Hermanos, a tortilla factory in Bushwick that also serves south-of-the-border standards using the fresh wraps. A flatbread made from corn or wheat, tortillas have been a staple since the Aztec civilization. Traditionally made completely by hand, and now in most cases by machine, tortillas have become one of the most popular flatbreads in the United States. While eating at Los Hermanos, you can watch the workers baking and bagging the tortillas. (Neighborhood artists line up early for the warm tortillas flying out of the kitchen.) The rest of the warm corn wraps (Los Hermanos makes corn tortillas exclusively) go straight into the kitchen to be partnered with one of many fillings. In our opinion, the chorizo is the best—the sausage is ground, grilled, and laced with chunks of potato and peppers. But all the food is healthy, tasty, and priced just right. Take your taco, taquito, or tostado to go, and stroll the nearby streets to view the best graffiti murals in Brooklyn. **9**

STAUBITZ MARKET

Staubitz Market is Brooklyn's entry into New York's best butcher shop sweepstakes: It consistently holds its own, offering meat, poultry, and game of the very highest quality, at about a third of Manhattan prices. The Staubitz family business, which has been owned by the McFadden family for forty years, has not changed much since it opened in 1917: creaking wooden screen door, tin ceiling, sawdust floor, antique light fixtures, and the original display cases (with updated refrigeration). The store windows and cashier's booth are trimmed with stained glass, and the wooden paneling gleams with the patina of time and use. Staubitz's meat is hand-cut under the supervision of John McFadden Jr. Along with conventional cuts, the shop offers an outstanding selection of wild poultry and game, including pheasant, partridge, quail, ostrich, and wild boar. If you are in a hurry, they also have a good grocery selection to go with the meat. Staubitz Market will take you back in time. **11**

STINKY BKLYN

By the time specialty cheese stores had started to conquer the city, the husband-and-wife duo of Patrick Watson and Michele Pravda had already made a name for themselves selling cheese. Pravda was a cheese fanatic and got great experience at Blue Hill. In 2010, Stinky opened in Brooklyn, followed by a second one in Manhattan. Stinky, on Smith Street between Butler and Baltic Streets, carries an extensive variety of cheeses from all around the world. Although the name definitely makes you think of cheese, Stinky is much more than a cheesemonger. The shop sells top-quality meat, including Dickson's Farmstand sausage, chicken, and lamb, and features a hand-carved-ham bar. Tasty prepared foods are among the offerings, including mac and cheese, chicken potpie, and panini. Stinky also boasts a coffee bar serving Brooklyn Roasting Company coffee; a newsstand; a cocktail section featuring syrups, mixers, and those ever-trendy bitters; plus gourmet goods—crackers, jams, and pickles—to complement the cheeses, from purveyors both near and far. The staff is incredibly friendly and knowledgeable and will answer as many questions as you have. Throwing a dinner party or a cocktail party? Stinky is a one-stop store for everything from cheese and charcuterie, crackers and breads, prepared foods, oil and vinegar, pickles, and jams—all of it good. **12**

DUMBO
BROOKLYN ROASTING COMPANY

In 1920, Jay Street was the location of the first coffee roaster in the United States. Before this innovation, coffee was sold in bulk, but the shelf life of the bean was quite short, so a new way to process the bean was in order. Enter John and Charlie Arbuckle: the mavericks who found a machine able to roast, prepare, and package coffee beans. By 1926, the Arbuckle clan was roasting twenty-five million pounds of beans every month. They acquired a boat and set it up as a café where Brooklynites and dockworkers could relax and enjoy a freshly brewed cup of coffee.

Today Jay Street is again involved in the coffee industry, thanks to Brooklyn Roasting Company, which makes its home in a big open warehouse, with lots of bags of beans piled up in the corners, an espresso lab, and a museum with a few antique coffee machines, some of which (believe it or not) still work. The espresso lab section of the facility is very welcoming: lots of easy chairs, counters with stools, lively conversation, and, of course, great coffee. No mistaking when Brooklyn Roasting's operations are in full force: The aroma fills the air. In the winter, stop by and warm up with a cappuccino or an espresso; in the summer you may prefer to pick up an iced coffee to go and relax in a garden at the end of the street on the grass facing Manhattan. We sampled many of the coffees, but our favorites were the Mexican Chiapas and the Brazil Sitío São Geraldo. The names alone are exciting, but the coffee buzz is even better. **13**

GOWANUS
FOUR & TWENTY BLACKBIRDS

Sisters Emily and Melissa Elsen hail from Hecla, South Dakota, where they learned pie-baking skills from their grandmother at the family's restaurant. Fortunately for East Coasters, the sisters moved to Brooklyn to open a pie shop of their own, Four & Twenty Blackbirds. Although their establishment may be a little hard to find, it's worth it to hone your Sherlock Holmes skills and get yourself there (preferably as many times as possible). The staff is friendly and willing to tell you everything—and quite poetically at that—about everything they bake. The handmade pies, sold whole or by the slice, are seasonal and dependent on locally grown ingredients. The apple rose and the pear crumble pies are among our favorites, but the standout is the salted caramel apple pie. It is one of those treats that your taste buds will remember long after you put down your fork. **14**

GREENPOINT
ACME SMOKED FISH

Chances are, if you've eaten smoked fish anywhere in the United States over the past thirty years, it was cured and smoked at Acme Smoked Fish in Greenpoint. The Brownstein family started smoking fish more than a hundred years ago, in 1905; Acme has become the largest family-owned commercial fish smoker in the country. Acme sells wholesale only, except on Fridays between 8 a.m. and 1 p.m., when it opens to the public and you can buy fish right out of the smoker at wholesale prices. Frozen and fresh fish from all over the world have been put through the Acme smoker. The variety of fish is enormous—wild Alaskan sockeye salmon, farm-raised Chilean salmon, mackerel, chubs from Lake Michigan, whitefish from Wisconsin, and, more recently, yellowtail tuna, bluefish, trout, and Alaskan black cod. First the fish are cured in a brine and sugar solution, varying in seasoning and intensity depending on the species. After curing for about a week, the fish is delivered to the smokers—cold smoking for salmon and sturgeon, hot smoking for chubs and herring—and smoked over apple- and cherrywood chips, with the smoke mixture adjusted to the desired flavor. Acme is out of the way, but worth a Friday morning trip across the East River. **15**

BAKERY RZESZOWSKA

Look for the no-nonsense sign on the corner that looks like it was designed by the Polish Ministry of Bakeries. The sweet smell of cheese babka wafts through the air as you approach the front door. This is Bakery Rzeszowska. The windows are packed with Polish cakes, pastries, and bread. If you want to know what they are, ask in Polish, because no one speaks English. If you don't speak Polish, listen to your eyes; if it looks good, it probably tastes good, especially the Danishes (cheese, apple, or strawberry), the poppy seed cake, and the famous babka. If you want to experience mouth-watering Polish pastry, and brush up on your Polish at the same time, this is the destination for you. **16**

14

SALTED CARAMEL APPLE PIE
Four & Twenty Blackbirds

SERVES 6 TO 8

The proprietors of this cozy bakery have given us one of the best apple pies in the world!

FOR THE DOUGH
2½ cups unbleached all-purpose flour
1 tablespoon granulated sugar
1 teaspoon salt
1 cup (2 sticks) cold unsalted butter, cut into ½-inch cubes
2 tablespoons apple cider vinegar combined with 1 cup water and some ice

FOR THE SALTED CARAMEL
1 cup granulated sugar
½ cup (1 stick) unsalted butter
½ cup heavy cream
1½ teaspoons flaky sea salt, such as Maldon

FOR THE APPLE FILLING
Juice of 2 lemons
5 to 6 medium to large apples (a mixture of Crispin, Granny Smith, and Cortland is nice)
¼ cup granulated sugar
⅓ cup raw cane sugar
¼ teaspoon ground cinnamon
¼ teaspoon ground allspice
⅛ teaspoon freshly grated nutmeg
2 or 3 dashes Angostura bitters
2 tablespoons unbleached all-purpose flour

FOR THE ASSEMBLY
1 large egg, beaten
1 teaspoon flaky sea salt, such as Maldon
About 1 teaspoon raw cane sugar

MAKE THE DOUGH

1 In a large bowl, whisk the flour, sugar, and salt together, then cut in the butter with a handheld pastry blender until the butter is in pea-size chunks. Be careful not to overwork the mixture during this step.

2 Slowly add 6 to 8 tablespoons of the vinegar–ice water mixture, just enough to make the dough come together. Gather the dough into a rough ball with your hands, again being careful not to overwork it: Aim to create a marbleized effect, so that the butter is still visible in streaks.

3 Divide the dough into two discs, wrap in plastic, and chill in the refrigerator for at least 1 hour. Meanwhile, make the salted caramel and apple filling.

MAKE THE SALTED CARAMEL

1 In a heavy saucepan, combine the sugar and ¼ cup water and cook over low heat until the sugar is just dissolved. Add the butter and bring to a low boil, stirring occasionally. Cook at a low boil until the mixture turns a deep, golden brown (almost copper) color. This process can take a while, depending on the heat source, but do keep an eye on it. If the caramel begins to smoke or turn very dark, it's burned and you'll have to start over.

2 As soon as the sugar and butter mixture has turned a copper color, remove from the heat and immediately add the cream. The mixture will bubble rapidly and steam. Be cautious, as the caramel will be very, very hot.

3 Return the pan to low heat, whisk the caramel together well, and sprinkle in the salt. Set aside.

MAKE THE APPLE FILLING

1 Put the lemon juice in a large bowl. Core, peel, and very thinly slice the apples whole (a mandoline works great for this). Toss the apples in the lemon juice to prevent them from browning and to add flavor. Add the granulated sugar and toss well to combine. Set aside.

2 In a large measuring cup or small bowl, mix together the raw sugar, cinnamon, allspice, nutmeg, bitters, and flour.

3 Drain the excess liquid from the apples. Sprinkle the spice mixture over the apples in the bowl. Use your hands to gently toss the apple slices so they're well coated with the spice mixture.

14

ASSEMBLE AND BAKE THE PIE

1 Preheat the oven to 375°F.

2 Unwrap one of the dough discs and roll it out on a lightly floured surface to about 1 inch thick. Fit it into a 9-inch pie plate.

3 Layer the apple filling in the bottom of the crust so that there are minimal gaps. Pour a generous amount of the salted caramel, but not all of it, over the layer of apples. Make a second layer of apples, then caramel, then a third layer of apples, then caramel again. Reserve a small portion of caramel to pour over the top crust.

4 Roll out the second dough disc and cut it into ¾-inch strips. Weave the strips over the top of the pie into a lattice design, attaching the ends to the edge of the bottom crust.

5 Flute the edge of the crust. Drizzle the reserved caramel on top. Brush with the beaten egg and lightly sprinkle the top with the sea salt and then the raw sugar.

6 Place the pie on a baking sheet larger than the pie pan (to prevent any caramel that bubbles over from burning on the bottom of your oven) and bake on the bottom rack of the oven for 20 minutes. Lower the oven temperature to 325°F, move the pie and baking sheet to the center rack, and bake for 25 to 35 minutes. Test the apples for doneness with a long toothpick or small knife. They should be just soft. Let cool on a wire rack for at least 1 hour, then slice and enjoy.

17

TEA-GLAZED MADELEINES

Bellocq Tea Atelier

MAKES 12

Madeleines alone are divine, but Bellocq tea glaze lends them an added dimension to enjoy with a cup of the atelier's fabulous tea. You will need a madeleine mold to make this recipe, but it's well worth the modest investment.

½ cup (1 stick) unsalted butter, plus more melted for pan

¾ cup all-purpose flour, plus more for dusting pan

½ cup cake flour

1 teaspoon aluminum-free baking powder

½ cup superfine sugar

3 large eggs, at room temperature

Pinch of salt

2 tablespoons darkish, full-flavored honey

2 teaspoons vanilla extract

2 teaspoons lemon zest

FOR THE MILK TEA GLAZE

1 cup whole milk

2 teaspoons Bellocq Queen's Guard tea

Pinch of salt

2 to 3 cups confectioners' sugar

1 Preheat the oven to 425°F with a baking rack set in the center of the oven.

BELLOCQ TEA ATELIER

Greenpoint is known for its warehouses and industrial buildings, housing the likes of a rope company, a lumberyard, and the well-known Eberhard Faber pencil company. It is a surprise to find, tucked away in one of these warehouses, one of the finest tea companies in the world. Bellocq, the award-winning tea company and purveyor of evocative artisan blends, has relocated its tea atelier to Greenpoint, Brooklyn, following the success of its Kings Road shop in London. The emporium, which offers a unique and evocative line of handcrafted tea blends, with seductive names such as Kikuya, Le Hammeau, and Noble Savage, also curates an inspiring selection of organic full-leaf teas.

Bellocq is refining the luxury tea business to suit the evolving and sophisticated taste of the modern client. Bellocq's founders, Heidi Johannsen Stewart, Michael Shannon, and Scott Stewart, joined creative forces to bring to life a shared aesthetic vision that captures their appreciation of traditional artisan work and a love of fine tea. The entrance is unassuming, but once you walk through the door it is a tea devotee's fantasy. The first room contains shelves lined with giant yellow canisters, the names of the teas written on tidy white labels. The wooden counter is laden with teapots and huge vases of fresh flowers. The back room could be in New Orleans: It's appointed with a beautiful cushy sofa, exotic wallpaper, and lots of ferns hanging in baskets. Call to make an appointment to visit and savor the tea. Each blend is made with high-quality leaves and other natural ingredients, and all of the tea is sourced from the best plantations. **17**

NASSAU MEAT MARKET

2 Melt the butter in a small saucepan over medium heat until the milk solids separate. Remove from the heat, skim the solids from the surface of the butter, and discard. Pour the remaining clarified butter into a clean bowl; set aside.

3 Sift together both flours and the baking powder; set aside.

4 Brush a madeleine mold with melted butter. Lightly dust it with flour and place the pan in the freezer to chill.

5 In the bowl of an electric mixer fitted with the whisk attachment, combine the superfine sugar, eggs, salt, honey, vanilla, and lemon zest. Beat on high until pale and thickened, about 5 minutes.

6 Using a large spatula, fold in the flour mixture in two or three additions. Then fold in the clarified butter until just incorporated. Cover the bowl and refrigerate the batter for at least 1 hour or overnight.

7 When you're ready to bake, spoon about 1 tablespoon of the batter into each chilled and prepared madeleine form. Do not spread the batter. Bake for 8 to 10 minutes, until golden and just set.

FOR THE MILK TEA GLAZE

1 While the madeleines cool, bring the milk to a simmer in a saucepan over medium heat. Remove from the heat, add the tea and salt, and cover; steep for 30 minutes.

2 Strain the tea-infused milk into a clean bowl. Stir in the confectioners' sugar, a little at a time, until you've reached your desired consistency.

3 Drizzle the scalloped side of each madeleine with the glaze, or gently dip them in.

Part of the Greenpoint section of Brooklyn is called New Poland. For an outsider, it might as well be a Warsaw suburb. Polish is the predominant language, and most of the stores feature signs in Polish and carry traditional Polish products. Nassau Meat Market is a superb Polish butcher shop. The line extends out the door and down the block as Polish residents wait, not so patiently, to order cold-smoked sausages. Inside, sausage hangs everywhere, dangling overhead like a carnivore's Calder sculpture. Every morning, Nassau's sausage and pierogi offerings are written on a large chalkboard. Nassau carries ten different varieties of sausage, including perfect kielbasa. Everything is prepared and smoked in the store. The smoke rooms are closed to the public, but the smell of woodsmoke wafts through the store. **18**

MIDWOOD
MANSOURA

King Farouk of Egypt was known for his insatiable appetite and demanding palate. Once upon a time, the Mansoura family were bakers for King Farouk and continually pleased him with their remarkable Middle Eastern pastries. After Farouk was deposed in 1954, the Mansouras relocated, first to Paris and then to the Sephardic Jewish community of Midwood, Brooklyn. Here they uphold family traditions and standards first established more than two hundred years ago when their family began baking in Syria. Today, a new generation of Mansouras will greet you warmly and take you on a tour of the amazing pastries piled high in the glass cases. The *barbora*, a honey-drenched semolina cake, is enchanting paired with espresso. The pistachio baklava, the *maamoul*, and the *loukoum*, with rose water and pistachios, are also delightful. One of the Mansouras' secrets is their deep knowledge of ingredients—where to find the best pistachios, apricots, and honey. We're inclined to suggest that Mansoura is the finest Middle Eastern bakery in New York. **19**

PARK SLOPE
BKLYN LARDER

Bklyn Larder is not just a cheese and provisions shop—it's at the center of the Brooklyn food revolution. Housed in an inviting, bright setting, with white tiles on the walls, a wooden floor, a big sausage-adorned rack, a soup station, and a large kitchen in the back, Bklyn Larder is a cornucopia of the best food purveyors, both local and worldwide.

The three owners, Sergio Hernandez, Andrew Feinberg, and Francine Stephens, each brought a different skill set to the operation, in addition to their shared passion for food. Hernandez came with an extensive knowledge of cheese. Feinberg contributes a "less is more" philosophy: He believes that "if a dish has three perfect ingredients, then it doesn't need anything else." Stephens has spent her entire professional career educating consumers, chefs, businesses, and community leaders about the means and benefits of an economy and environment improved by purchasing locally grown foods and products. Since we were there, we tried the tuna, the egg salads, and the meatballs; they were perfectly executed. The cheese and cured meat counter can rival Barthélémy cheese shop in Paris. The grocery section is a lesson in quality: jams, pastas, olive oils, snacks, sugar, beer, and more. In the refrigerated section, you'll find yogurt, homemade ice cream, pâtés . . . plus a daily selection of prepared foods to take away or sit at the counter and enjoy. Everything at Bklyn Larder is a winner! **20**

DOWN TO EARTH MARKETS

Down to Earth Markets brings two kinds of vendors together: area farmers and food purveyors who source locally. It operates in Brooklyn as well as Manhattan, Queens, Westchester County, and Rockland County. We visited the Park Slope market a few times and it became clear it was a favorite market of families in the area. All the vendors know one another and their regular customers by name, and, more important, they are eager to help customers understand their products. You might actually spend more time conversing with the vendors than shopping. To whet your appetite, here are a few of the vendors. **21**

Calcutta Kitchens

Visit Aditi Goswami's stand and she will tell you stories about her childhood in India, where food was a way to express love and care, and to work with nature's bounty. She is best known for her Indian simmer sauces, which will turn any main ingredient into an instant meal. Prepared sauces require fastidious preparation and often a long cooking time, and Goswami makes hers with fresh ingredients, passion, and a lot of energy. In this case, the label is your blueprint to your meal: It provides a detailed explanation on how to prepare meat, fish, vegetables, tofu, and even pizza with the sauce. Try the Makhani Tikka Simmer Sauce, a mild creamy tomato sauce, or the Coconut Coriander Simmer Sauce. Both are delicious.

Demi Olive Oil

The story goes something like this: John was a fireman and Demitria cooked for him; he loved her cooking and they got married. John quit his job to learn about the olive oil that made Demitria's cooking so irresistible, and now they own an olive oil farm in Greece and import their olive oil, which they sell here. It's fresh and very smooth, with a peppery note.

Sohha Savory Yogurt

Finding a good homemade yogurt in Brooklyn can be an adventure. You can buy a yogurt machine or find a farmer friend who can bring you raw milk and a starter and attempt to make your own yogurt . . . or you can go directly to Sohha and buy the creamiest yogurt you will ever eat. Choose from original or tangy: It's made from locally sourced whole milk, probiotic cultures, and sea salt.

FLEISHER'S CRAFT BUTCHERY

In 2004 we heard that the best butcher in New York State was in Kingston, so we drove upstate to meet the couple behind the butchery: Joshua and Jessica Applestone. A few years later, we didn't have to drive to purchase their carefully selected and masterfully cut grass-fed meat, but visited their Park Slope butcher shop instead, where we received an equally warm welcome. From our trek upstate to the flagship store we remembered the story of how the Fleisher family sources such consistently superb meat: They've developed personal relationships with the best local farmers and follow the animals, so they know what they've been fed and how they've been treated and harvested. These days the company is much bigger, with five locations and a butcher school that offers a twelve-week apprenticeship. The Park Slope store is sparkling clean and the staff is passionate about their product and eager to share their skills. Large refrigerated cases display an impeccable selection of meat, all of which is locally sourced and hormone- and antibiotic-free. Whether you take home the roasted chicken, aged steaks, bacon, sausages, or pork belly rillettes, you will never regret a trip to Fleisher's. Here, everything is perfect, including the butchers. **22**

O LIVE BROOKLYN

When Greg Bernarducci and his wife, Elisabeth Weiss, opened O Live, a shop featuring a large, fresh selection of single-varietal extra-virgin olive oil and aged balsamic vinegar on tap, they did not imagine that their customers would range from Orthodox Jews to Brooklyn hipsters. They dispense their wares from shiny metal kettles that line the store. Cups provided below each variety of oil and vinegar allow you to taste before you buy—and the tasting is the fun part. To help you along, descriptions ranging from nutty, spicy, fragrant, or muddy to herbaceous, earthy, or smoky grace each offering, and the aroma becomes apparent as you sip. Some taste like hay, pepper, or tea leaf, others like lime or mint. O Live sells more than a dozen kinds of olive oil, eleven infused ones, twenty-three kinds of balsamic vinegar, and five specialty oils. Our favorite is the ginger-infused olive oil. The store has become the premier olive oil source for professional and home chefs, organic food lovers, and foodies who seek the highest-quality products. Olive oil is best when used fresh, so the harvest date is posted on each oil. On our next visit, we're thinking of taking along a loaf of bread and staying awhile. **23**

PROSPECT HEIGHTS
AMPLE HILLS CREAMERY

This popular ice creamery opened only a few years ago, when Brian Smith decided to take a break from writing science fiction movies and turned to making the most delicious, hand-made, all-natural, small-batch ice cream in Brooklyn's Prospect Heights. The Ample Hills shop is a haven for children, with charming wall drawings and a big blackboard displaying the daily flavors—and adults can't resist the fun atmosphere, either. But the big attraction (besides the ice cream itself) is the bicycle that churns the cream right before your eyes in the front window. Popular flavors include Chocolate Milk and Cookies, Toffee Bar Crunch, Vanilla Malted, Cotton Candy, Lemon Sky, Ooey Gooey Butter Cake, and Nanatella (banana and Nutella). **24**

RED HOOK
BAKED

Baked is the creation of Matt Lewis and Renato Poliafito, two former administrators who realized they shared a passion for American bakery comfort food, resulting in the opening of this popular bakery in Red Hook. Their clever sensibilities are reflected in both the decor and the baked goods—updated and retooled renditions of nostalgic American sweet treats. Lewis and Poliafito are hands-on owners who have ensured the highest-quality products for the benefit of all their customers by personally eating through thousands of desserts. The menu changes seasonally, but some of the more popular cake flavors include Aunt Sassy's Pistachio Surprise, citrus passion fruit, carrot, and caramel apple. **25**

CACAO PRIETO

Cacao Prieto was founded by Daniel Prieto Preston, an aerospace engineer whose family has been farming organic cacao and sugarcane in the Dominican Republic for more than a hundred years. Cacao Prieto creates artisanal chocolates from end to end—from the single-origin Dominican organic pods to beans to bars. The building that houses this combination chocolate factory and liquor distillery, with a retail shop and cocktail bar thrown in for good measure, is one of the most beautiful redbrick buildings in Red Hook. Inside, the imposing copper machinery does the hard work while antique wooden cabinets hold lovely displays of confections and bottles of liquor. A tour of the building reveals the process of making fine chocolate in detail. The factory shop showcases perfectly handcrafted bonbons in twelve enticing flavors, as well as dark chocolate bars with fruits and nuts, jars of nuts and cacao spreads, and coffee liqueurs. **26**

RED HOOK LOBSTER POUND

The live lobsters at the Red Hook Lobster Pound arrive directly from Maine, and the shop has become a destination for lobster lovers. Neighborhood customers and chefs make this their go-to for the freshest lobster in Brooklyn. The highlight of the store is the giant scale and the two lobster tanks. Grab your lobster, weigh it, and the shop will cook it for you in its kitchen. While you wait, tuck into one of the lobster rolls—Maine style, tossed with mayonnaise; Connecticut style, served hot with butter and lemon; or Tuscan style, tossed in a basil vinaigrette—and eat it fresh next door in the indoor picnic-style dining room.

There are many reasons for the Lobster Pound's success. Owners Ralph Gorham and Susan Povich are passionate about their business, and their focus is exclusively lobster. This single-mindedness has made it possible for them to get the best-quality fresh lobsters from Maine. Their recipes, including Lobster Mac and Cheese and the Cobbster Salad, also have been carefully perfected, and the broth they use to cook the lobster adds to the unique character of the meat. Here the mayo is homemade, and the drawn butter is high quality. If you cannot make the trip to Red Hook, look out for the Lobster Pound's food truck, Big Red, in Manhattan; the logo is unmistakable—red lobster claws hooked to the back of a blue truck. **27**

STEVE'S AUTHENTIC KEY LIME PIES

There are key lime pies, and then there are Steve's Authentic Key Lime Pies. Steve Tarpin started baking pies for family and friends as a hobby more than thirty years ago, and eventually began delivering them to restaurants and stores around New York City. Since the nineties he's had a thriving storefront in the Red Hook section of Brooklyn, not far from Fairway. The pier along New York Harbor where the shop operates is a bit difficult to find, and it feels like something out of the Florida Keys, but find it you must. The ingredients for Steve's pies are simple: fresh-squeezed lime juice from authentic key limes; they're about half the size of regular limes with a lot more bite. The juice is mixed into a custard, then poured into a crisp graham cracker crust. Enjoy a slice of key lime pie in Steve's waterside garden along the pier, or take a pie home. The pies come in three different sizes and keep well in the freezer. **28**

LOBSTER MAC AND CHEESE

Red Hook Lobster Pound

SERVES 8

Everyone loves macaroni and cheese, and this recipe includes the meat of five lobsters cooked in a lobster stock, making for an elegant version.

FOR THE QUICK LOBSTER STOCK

2 leeks, washed, trimmed, and coarsely chopped

3 sprigs fresh thyme

2 teaspoons sea salt

1 teaspoon Old Bay Seasoning

1 cup white wine

5 (1½-pound) live lobsters

FOR THE MAC AND CHEESE

6 tablespoons unsalted butter, plus 2 tablespoons for the topping

⅓ cup all-purpose flour

4 cups whole milk

1 (14-ounce) package elbow macaroni or gobetti

6 ounces Gruyère cheese, grated

3 ounces mild cheddar cheese, grated

10 ounces Asiago cheese, grated

8 ounces mascarpone cheese

½ pinch freshly grated nutmeg

Salt and freshly ground black pepper

1½ cups panko bread crumbs

2 tablespoons lemon zest

1 tablespoon chopped fresh thyme

PREPARE THE LOBSTER STOCK

1 In a large pot, bring 4 inches of water to a rolling boil. Add the leeks, thyme, salt, Old Bay, and wine and boil for 2 to 3 minutes. Add the lobsters, cover the pot, and keep at a rolling boil for 10 minutes. Remove the cooked lobsters and drain them into a container that can catch their juices. (You can crack the lobsters now if you want to encourage more juice to be released.)

2 Add the lobster juices to the broth, then strain the broth through a fine-mesh sieve or cheesecloth and return it to the pot. Reduce over medium heat until you have about 6 cups of stock.

MAKE THE MAC AND CHEESE

1 Preheat the oven to 350°F.

2 Melt 6 tablespoons of the butter in a medium saucepan, sift in the flour, and cook over low heat for 1 minute. Heat the milk with 1¼ cups of the reduced lobster stock and add it slowly to the butter and flour mixture, then cook over low heat for 10 minutes, stirring, until the sauce has thickened. When the sauce is thick enough to coat a spoon, add the Gruyère, cheddar, Asiago, mascarpone, and nutmeg. Season with salt and pepper. Remove from the heat and let rest.

27

3 Meanwhile, boil the noodles in the remaining reduced stock (add a little water if you need more liquid) for 3 minutes, until half cooked.

4 Pick the meat from the lobsters (tail, claw, knuckle, and bodies if you are so inclined); rinse off the tomalley. Clean and chop the tails into ¾-inch pieces. Do not chop the claws. Drain the noodles, mix in the cheese sauce and lobster meat, and check the seasoning. Grease a gratin pan with nonstick cooking spray and pour in the noodle mixture, spreading out the lobster evenly in the pan. (I use whatever baking dish the mac and cheese fills nicely to the top.) Set aside.

5 Melt the remaining 2 tablespoons butter in a pan over medium heat. Add the panko, lemon zest, and thyme and cook for a few minutes while stirring to bring out the flavor. Spread the topping evenly over the mac and cheese mixture.

6 Bake for 40 minutes. Let cool a few minutes before serving.

WILLIAMSBURG
BAKERI

Bakeri was opened in 2009 by Nina Brondmo, a Norwegian, and Pablo Arganaraz, her Argentinean husband. Frequented by locals, artists, and musicians, this charming spot, situated in the Williamsburg section of Brooklyn, boasts a true New York City café vibe. As one would expect from a Scandinavian-owned establishment, the place is welcoming, with glass-fronted oak cabinets full of fresh pastries and cakes. The staff, in blue jumpsuits with scarves wrapped around their heads, channels an adorable 1950s vibe. There are a few tables outside in front of the store, a long table inside, and an enchanting garden in the back. The high-quality goods are baked and sold on the same day. Brondmo excels at *skolebrød*, a Norwegian sweet dough pastry with cream and coconut that is not to be missed, but if that doesn't do it for you, then try a slice of the caramelized pear and almond coffee cake, the brioche, the strawberry pear scone, or the ham and cheese roll. We sampled just about everything, but our favorite was the banana-size biscotti with nuts, raisins, and chocolate chips. This is a Norwegian pastry shop at its best, so let yourself be transported by the smell of homemade traditional Scandinavian goods all day long, right in the middle of Williamsburg. **29**

MARLOW & DAUGHTERS

Marlow & Daughters is one of those food purveyors that, once visited, you wish were in your neighborhood. The store is a ringer for a traditional French grocery and could easily be mistaken for a movie set. A charming man named Doug welcomed us to the store and explained every section to us. It is a whole animal butcher shop that specializes in locally and sustainably raised meat, poultry, and handmade sausages, as well as in-house charcuterie, seasonal produce, prepared foods, and many other specialty grocery items.

Fruit and vegetables are seasonal and almost always from farms within two hundred miles of the shop; some are sourced from just a mile away. The vegetables are sometimes as quirky and unique as the staff. Grocery products are a well-curated mix from New York City–based purveyors, small-batch artisanal food outfits in Europe, and other items from companies using sustainable and ethical business practices. This is more than just a grocery—it is an education in the way food should be prepared and consumed. When you walk into the shop, chances are the aroma of simmering broth will greet you—the perfect thing to get your day started on a cold morning. **30**

MAST BROTHERS CHOCOLATE

Rick and Michael Mast share a passion for making the perfect chocolate bar. They buy only the best cocoa beans from Madagascar, Ecuador, Venezuela, and the Dominican Republic. They care deeply about their craft, down to the colorful, eye-catching wrappers inspired by wallpaper that enclose their many varieties of chocolate bars. To maintain the integrity of the chocolate, the brothers make it in small batches, following a strict method. The beans are slowly roasted, broken up by hand, winnowed, stone-ground, and left to rest for two to three weeks. This system creates perfect, glossy, delicious chocolate in several flavors. Purists should try the Dominican Republic 70 percent organic dark chocolate (with almonds, sea salt, olive oil, or serrano peppers). From there, graduate to the 72 percent (with hazelnuts or cocoa nibs) or, better still, the Venezuelan 81 percent. Visit the warehouse in Williamsburg, in an old spice factory, and watch as the unhusked cocoa nibs are ground. Chocolate lovers, tourists, and the curious invade every weekend and always leave with a chocolate bar, a cookie, a tart, or the Mast Brothers cookbook. These are very special chocolate bars: It will be hard to choose just one flavor, so buy a few and savor every morsel. **31**

THE MEAT HOOK AND THE BROOKLYN KITCHEN

The Meat Hook and the Brooklyn Kitchen are two separate stores that opened in 2010 under the same roof in a redbrick warehouse in Williamsburg. The address is hard to find but worth the hunt—this is a must-see destination for any foodie. The Brooklyn Kitchen, which occupies the second floor of the warehouse, is filled with great kitchen supplies, knives, pots, pans, utensils, and cookbooks, as well as a large section devoted to craft beer. The kitchen on the ground floor next to the butcher holds ever-popular cooking classes.

The Meat Hook, a butcher, has a rear wall with a hanging display of knives that could be a museum exhibition. The counter is open, providing customers with an unobstructed view as butchers, both male and female, cut up beef, pork, and chicken. This whole-animal butcher shop specializes in local meat from small family farms in New York state. All of the beef is 100-percent grass fed, and the pork and lamb are raised on wide-open green pastures. Since our last visit, The Meat Hook has moved out and now has its own store as well as a sandwich shop, both in Williamsburg. **32**

CORN PUDDING

The Brooklyn Kitchen

SERVES 4 TO 6

This recipe takes corn to a creamy and delicious level. Serve it as a side dish.

4 tablespoons unsalted butter

2 large eggs

2 teaspoons kosher salt or sea salt

2 tablespoons sugar

½ teaspoon freshly ground
   black pepper

2 cups whole milk

½ cup all-purpose flour

2½ cups fresh corn off the cob
   (from 4 ears)

1 Preheat the oven to 350°F. Place the butter in a 9 by 13-inch casserole and melt it in the oven.

2 In a medium bowl, beat together the eggs, salt, sugar, pepper, milk, and flour. When the egg mixture is smooth, stir in the corn.

3 Remove the casserole dish from the oven and pour the corn batter into the casserole. Bake for 1 hour, or until the pudding has set and is browned on the top. Serve warm.

33

MOMOFUKU MILK BAR

Started by award-winning pastry chef and owner Christina Tosi in 2008, this chain of sweet spots has nothing less than a cult following. The Brooklyn location is small and charming, with an oversize blackboard listing all the available baked goods. These include the infamous Crack Pie, with its toasted oat crust, gooey buttery sugar and cream filling, which is as addictive as the street drug it's playfully named after. The compost cookie (studded with pretzels, potato chips, ground coffee, oats, and butterscotch and chocolate chips) and the cornflake cookie (featuring cornflakes, marshmallows, and chocolate chips) are the stuff that legends are made of. The soft-serve ice cream is light and creamy, and it comes in outrageous but delectable flavors like cereal milk, blueberry miso, and guava horchata. There are small cakes, big cakes, the famous birthday cake—the Milk Bar's take on a funfetti cake—and wedding cakes. Momofuku Milk Bar is a dessert world unto its own, and Tosi is the pied piper of sweet imagination. **33**

CRACK PIE
Momofuku Milk Bar

SERVES 8

Christina Tosi is the genius behind Crack Pie. It is definitely addictive!

FOR THE OAT COOKIE
½ cup (1 stick) unsalted butter, at room temperature
⅓ cup firmly packed light brown sugar
3 tablespoons granulated sugar
1 large egg yolk
½ cup all-purpose flour
1½ cups old-fashioned rolled oats
⅛ teaspoon baking powder
Pinch of baking soda
½ teaspoon kosher salt

FOR THE OAT COOKIE CRUST
1 tablespoon firmly packed light brown sugar
¼ teaspoon kosher salt
4 tablespoons unsalted butter, melted, plus more if needed

FOR THE FILLING
1½ cups granulated sugar
¾ cups firmly packed light brown sugar
¼ cup dry milk powder
¼ cup corn powder
1½ teaspoons kosher salt
1 cup (2 sticks) unsalted butter, melted
¾ cup heavy cream
½ teaspoon pure vanilla extract
8 large egg yolks

Confectioners' sugar, for dusting

MAKE THE OAT COOKIE

1 Preheat the oven to 350°F. Spray a baking sheet with nonstick cooking spray (such as Pam) and line it with parchment paper, or just line the pan with a silicone baking mat.

2 In the bowl of a stand mixer fitted with the paddle attachment, cream the butter and sugars on medium-high speed for 2 to 3 minutes, until fluffy and pale yellow. Scrape down the sides of the bowl with a spatula. With the mixer on low speed, add the egg yolk, then increase the speed to medium-high and beat for 1 to 2 minutes, until the sugar granules are completely dissolved and the mixture is pale white.

3 With the mixer on low speed, add the flour, oats, baking powder, baking soda, and salt.

Mix for 1 minute, until the dough comes together and any remnants of dry ingredients have been incorporated. The dough will be a slightly fluffy, fatty mixture in comparison with your average cookie dough. Scrape down the sides of the bowl.

4 Plop the cookie dough in the center of the prepared pan and, with a spatula, spread it out until it is ¼ inch thick. The dough won't end up covering the entire pan; this is okay. Bake for 15 minutes, or until the cookie is caramelized on top and puffed slightly but set firmly. Let cool completely before proceeding. The cookie can be made up to one week ahead, wrapped well in plastic, and refrigerated.

MAKE THE OAT COOKIE CRUST

1 Break up the oat cookie into large pieces. Put the broken-up cookie, brown sugar, and salt in a food processor and pulse until the cookie is broken down and has the consistency of wet sand.

2 Transfer the mixture to a bowl, add the butter, and knead until moist enough to form into a ball. If it is not moist enough to do so, melt an additional 1 to 1½ tablespoons butter and knead it in.

3 Divide the dough evenly between two 10-inch pie pans. Using your fingers and the palms of your hands, press the dough firmly into each pie pan, making sure the bottom and sides of the pan are evenly covered. Use the pie shells immediately, or wrap well in plastic and store at room temperature for up to 5 days or in the fridge for up to 2 weeks.

MAKE THE FILLING

1 Put the sugars, dry milk powder, corn powder, and salt in the bowl of a stand mixer fitted with the paddle attachment and mix on low speed until thoroughly combined. Add the butter and beat for 2 to 3 minutes, until all the dry ingredients are moist.

Add the cream and vanilla and continue mixing on low speed for 2 to 3 minutes, until any white streaks from the cream have completely disappeared into the mixture. Scrape down the sides of the bowl with a spatula.

2 Add the egg yolks, beating them into the mixture on low speed just to combine; be careful to not aerate the mixture, but mix until it is glossy and homogenous. Use the filling right away or store in an airtight container in the refrigerator for up to 1 week.

When ready to bake, preheat the oven to 350°F.

BAKE THE PIE

1 Put both pie shells on a baking sheet. Divide the filling evenly between the crusts; the filling should fill them three-quarters of the way full. Bake for 15 minutes, until the pies are golden brown on top but still very jiggly. Open the oven door and lower the oven temperature to 325°F. Depending on your oven it may take 5 minutes or longer for the oven to cool to the new temperature. Keep the pies in the oven during this process.

2 When the oven reaches 325°F, close the door and bake the pies for 5 minutes longer. The pies should still be jiggly in the bull's-eye center but

not around the outer edges. (If the filling is still too jiggly, leave the pies in the oven for an additional 5 minutes or so.)

Gently take the pan of crack pies out of the oven and transfer them to a wire rack to cool to room temperature. Freeze the pies for at least 3 hours, or overnight, to condense the filling for a dense final product—freezing is the signature technique, and the result is a perfectly executed crack pie. If not serving the pies right away, cover tightly in plastic wrap.

3 In the refrigerator they will keep for 5 days; in the freezer they will keep for 1 month. Transfer the pies from the freezer to the refrigerator to defrost for at least 1 hour before slicing them. Serve your crack pie cold! Decorate with confectioners' sugar, either by sifting it through a fine-mesh sieve or dispatching pinches with your fingers.

QUEENS

Geographically adjacent to Brooklyn, Queens is the easternmost and largest in area of New York City's five boroughs. It is the site of the city's major airports—JFK and LaGuardia—and home to the U.S. Open tennis championship.

The area now called Queens was first occupied by Native Americans, then settled by the Dutch and later by English Puritans, who named the area after Catherine of Braganza, the Portuguese wife of Charles II, the Scottish king of England. This founding potpourri of settlers only hints at the melting pot that constitutes present-day Queens. Strolling its avenues, you are likely to hear Spanish, Chinese, Korean, Italian, Greek, Russian, Creole, an assortment of Indian languages, Portuguese, and probably some English. And every one of those languages is represented by more than one food store. Its neighborhoods are as diverse a patchwork of culinary traditions as you will find anywhere in the world. This is the borough with the greatest influx of new immigrants, and housing is relatively cheap compared to most of Manhattan and Brooklyn. When you change neighborhoods in Queens, you change cultures. You can get from Cali to Delhi, or Seoul to Athens, in the blink of an eye. These communities tend to have large first- and second-generation immigrant populations, so the food stores have an ethnic authenticity that is hard to find anywhere else.

AL-SHAM SWEETS & PASTRIES

Al-Sham is the creation of two Palestinian-Jordanian brothers, Hassam and Talal, third-generation bakers who were raised in Russia. In 2009, they set up shop in Astoria and it has since become a thriving neighborhood bakery, always filled with Middle Eastern gastronomic wonders, including some of the best pastry in the borough. It is bustling with commerce from morning to night, and the brothers are extremely friendly and eager to explain each pastry. The baklava is notable; the generously apportioned fillings include pistachio (a bestseller), walnut, cinnamon, and chocolate—and you can hear the crunch of the flaky phyllo dough as it crumbles with your first bite. The honey cake is outstanding, and the cookies are even better. We love the sesame circles: crunchy, nutty, and not too sweet. If you aren't familiar with the names of all the items in the bakery case, not to worry—just point to something, and there's a good chance you will love it. **1**

ANDRE'S HUNGARIAN STRUDELS & PASTRIES

Vienna gave the world apple strudel and psychoanalysis, which leads us to ask—which is more therapeutic, fifty minutes on the couch or a slice of a warm apple strudel? After visiting Andre's, we lean toward the strudel. Andre Heimann has been at this same Queens Boulevard location since the 1940s. We watched Heimann make apple strudel and marveled at his skill and patience.

The high-gluten dough starts as a three-by-two-foot square, which Heimann stretches, rolls, and presses by hand until it is as large and thin as a queen-size flat sheet. The dough rests on a special table that gently blows air underneath it, causing the dough to billow gently above the tabletop. When the dough is nearly transparent, he trims it to fit a six-by-four-foot table. He then runs a long, thick line of filling about a foot from one edge of the dough and rolls the dough until the entire sheet is wrapped tightly around the filling. The strudels emerge golden brown from the oven with an extraordinarily light and flaky crust. Andre's strudels contain apple, cheese, cherry, or poppy seed fillings, so if you are still considering psychoanalysis, first take a subway ride to Andre's bakery. He might save you a fortune in analyst's bills. **2**

ARTOPOLIS

If you haven't been to Greece but would like to see what it looks like and experience its baked goods, then step into Artopolis—you'll feel like you have just landed in Athens. Artopolis is an odyssey of confectionaries, a cornucopia of pastries, breads, cakes, tarts, pies, and other Mediterranean delights that will take your taste buds from Athens to Astoria. The shop is run by natives of Kefalonia and Ithaca, and the recipes come from their families and friends.

The baklava is outstanding but our favorite is the *galaktoboureko*: layers of light phyllo dough with a Greek cream filling. We also enjoyed the *kourabiedes*, or walnut sugar cookies, used to celebrate births, weddings, and birthdays, and the turnovers known as *skaltsoni*, a specialty from Crete that happens to be vegan, featuring a stone-ground whole wheat pastry with marmalade, cherries, almonds, and nutmeg filling. The pastries, pies, and cookies will leave you with dreams of throwing a Greek wedding, but don't leave without purchasing some of the celebratory almonds in about ten flavors and different colors. And, just in case your limit for sweets hasn't been challenged, try the *diples*: vodka-spiked fried dough dipped in honey. *Oopah!* **3**

BAKLAVA

Artopolis

Baklava is one of those desserts that is always memorable. The delicate dough and the nutty honey filling will keep you coming back for more.

FOR THE SYRUP

2 cups sugar

2½ tablespoons honey

Juice of ½ lemon

2 small strips lemon peel

3 small cinnamon sticks

FOR THE BAKLAVA

1 cup raw almonds, crushed to small pieces

1 cup raw walnuts, crushed to small pieces

2 tablespoons sugar

2 teaspoons ground cinnamon

20 sheets store-bought frozen phyllo dough, thawed according to the package directions

¾ cup (1½ sticks) unsalted butter, melted

Preheat the oven to 350°F.

MAKE THE SYRUP

In a saucepan, combine the sugar, honey, lemon juice and peel, cinnamon sticks, and 1 cup water and bring to a boil. Lower the heat and simmer for 5 minutes, then remove from the heat, strain, and let cool.

MAKE THE BAKLAVA

1 Toss together the almonds, walnuts, sugar, and cinnamon in a bowl.

2 Cut the phyllo sheets to fit in an 8 by 12-inch baking dish. Keep them open, flat on a work surface, covered by a damp cotton cloth to prevent them from drying out.

3 Brush the bottom of the 8 by 12-inch baking dish with melted butter. Cover immediately with a sheet of phyllo. Brush the top of the sheet with butter and continue the process, layering phyllo sheets and buttering them, until you have a neat stack of ten sheets lining the bottom of the dish.

4 Spread half the nut mixture over the phyllo, patting it down firmly and spreading it evenly. Cover with another two sheets of phyllo, buttering each one as you go. Scatter the rest of the nuts evenly over the top and press down gently.

5 Finally, add the last eight sheets of phyllo dough, one by one, buttering each one as you go and finishing with butter on top.

6 Using a small sharp knife, cut the baklava on the diagonal into 2½-inch diamonds. Sprinkle a few drops of cold water over the top to prevent curling.

7 Bake for 25 to 30 minutes, until lightly golden on top. Remove from the oven and pour half the syrup all over the baklava. Wait for the baklava to absorb the syrup, then pour on the rest. Let cool completely before serving.

INTHIRA THAI MARKET

In a nondescript neighborhood in Queens stands a jewel in the rough. Plastic chairs and a plastic tree border the entryway. There is no air conditioning, so the fans work overtime. In short, it's a quick way to experience Thailand's hot, humid weather without the long flight. The owner, a beautiful, petite ex-housewife who named the store after herself, was at the cash register with a relative when we arrived, chatting in Thai. But after a few minutes, they warmed up to us and switched to English, sharing an informative and delightful overview of the store's history and offerings. In 2012, Inthira decided to launch a real Thai grocery store, and soon her place became one of the go-to groceries for New York City's top chefs. On the shelves, you will find many choices of noodles, plus rows and rows of sauces and condiments, including tamarind paste, curry, chile paste, and coconut milk, fermented bean curd, and an abundance of spices. If you are looking for fresh Thai veggies, you've come to the right place—Thai basil, sweet basil, and hard-to-find holy basil are all here, along with Thai eggplant, Thai acacia (it doesn't smell great raw, but it's delicious once cooked), bird's-eye chile peppers, galangal (this scary-looking root is a popular seasoning in Thai cooking, often used interchangeably with ginger), and fresh lemongrass. This tiny store is positively packed with authentic Thai ingredients. If you come at the end the day, do not miss having dinner at SriPraPhai Thai restaurant directly across the street. **4**

OMEGA WINES AND SPIRITS

Plaza Market is a small enclave of Greek food and culture, home to a butcher selling the best goat meat for your next barbecue, Artopolis bakery, the House of Greece grocery store, and Omega Wines and Spirits. Outside there is a small courtyard where you can sip a Greek coffee, but close your eyes and imagine you're at a café in Athens, enjoying the traditional anise-flavored aperitif ouzo. Or visit Omega Wines and Spirits to re-create the experience at home; the shop offers an outstanding selection of wines and liquors from Greece, including ouzo (it's revered by the Greeks).

The Greeks have been aware of the nutritional value of wine for the past four thousand years and have been making wines ever since. I urge you to explore: At this well-stocked wine shop, you will find an array of options from all regions of Greece—including the Aegean Islands, Epirus, Macedonia, the Peloponnese, Sterea Hellas, and Thessaly. Omega Wines and Spirits also offers a large selection of liquors (Tsipouro, Zivania, Tsikoudia, and more), and of course several varieties of ouzo. (Warning: Ouzo has quite a high alcohol content, about 40 percent, so do not forget to add water and ice!) The owner was very charming and gave us interesting insight into Greek wines and spirits. **5**

PATEL BROTHERS

In Queens the short drive from Flushing to Jackson Heights is akin to a quick and easy trip from East Asia to the Indian subcontinent. When you reach Thirty-Seventh Street in Jackson Heights, suddenly the store signs are in Hindi, Bollywood music blares from storefront speakers, and incense fills the air. Visit this neighborhood on a sunny day; you'll be dazzled by the vivid colors of women's saris and jewelry, and the elegance of the men in their high-collared white suits. Indians, Pakistanis, Sikhs, and Bangladeshi live side by side in this tightly packed community, and the food stores reflect each of these cultures. Patel Brothers is the largest food store in the neighborhood. Known for exotic chutneys, masalas, and an extensive selection of frozen prepared foods, it also sells large bags of rice, an incredible variety of spices, and fresh fruits and vegetables. Everyone working in the store is ready to answer questions, explaining unfamiliar food items with a big smile and a bit of laughter. **6**

游水 泥鳅
LIVE MUDFISH
$16.99/LB
skyFOODS 晶晶超市

SKY FOODS

Sky Foods is not easy to find. You will have to enter the brand-new mall in Flushing and go downstairs to reach the 36,000-square-foot supermarket: a lesson in East meet West, and the most comprehensive supermarket in the city for those who are looking for a crash course in Asian food. At the entrance to each aisle is a large sign listing what is found in that row. These are organized by region—Japanese, Chinese, Korean, Thai, Filipino foods— or by type of product: herbs, seaweed, fungus/dried mushrooms, salt, sugar, grains, fresh noodles, tofu/bean curd, soy sauce, vinegar, cooking wine, sesame oil, and preserved pickles, along with an array of sweets that rivals any candy store. In the back of the supermarket you will find the fresh fish department with live fish in tanks. Yes, Asians like to see the fish harvested before their eyes. They are not big fans of fillets but like buying and preparing the whole fish. Be ready for belt fish, jellyfish, catfish, soft shell turtles, eels, and other possibly unfamiliar things from the sea . . . there is also a meat section with a butcher cutting to order. Allow yourself ample time: You may need a few hours to take in all that this mega supermarket has to offer. **7**

SUBZI MANDI

This Indian grocery store, situated on a very busy corner in Jackson Heights, specializes in fruits and vegetables, some of which require explanations— which the owners are delighted to give. Take a pad and a pencil: We asked for a recipe and only looked up from our writing thirty minutes later. Some of our favorite new vegetables here are Chinese okra, Indian karela (a bitter gourd), unusual chiles, and long beans, plus lots of different lettuces, all a great detour from the usual broccoli and spinach. We also picked up some green cardamom that you can use to perfume your sweet rice, meat dishes, or chai tea. **8**

FETA
KEFALONIAS
$7.79 PER LB

AVGOLEMONO SOUP
Titan Foods

SERVES 4 TO 6

This is a traditional Greek pasta and chicken soup that can be served warm or cold. The people at Titan Foods told us that it's a must at any Greek wedding. *Oopah!*

7 cups chicken stock
1 cup orzo pasta
3 large eggs
2 lemons
Salt and freshly ground black pepper

1 In a large saucepan, bring the stock to a boil, then add the pasta and cook for 5 minutes.

2 In a small bowl, beat the eggs until foamy with 1 tablespoon water and the juice of one of the lemons.

3 Pour 1 tablespoon of the hot stock into the bowl; repeat this six times.

4 Remove the saucepan from the heat and pour the egg mixture from the bowl over the stock; stir very well and remove from the heat. Do not reheat the soup.

5 Transfer the soup to a serving bowl and add salt and pepper. Slice the remaining lemon and put the slices on the top of the soup. Serve immediately.

TITAN FOODS

In Greek mythology the leader of the Titans was Kronos, god of agriculture and the harvest. This aptly named Greek supermarket is the largest of its kind in North America. Titan offers a wide choice of distinctive, tangy Greek yogurt and the largest selection of anchovies this side of the Mediterranean—more than twenty varieties. Visit the feta bar, bakery, and olive bar and spend some time choosing from the display of powerful and pungent Greek olive oils. Be sure to pick up one of Titan's prepared seasoning mixes; it'll add great flavor to your next family barbecue. Many of the excellent Greek products sold here are exclusive to Titan, the culinary giant of Astoria. **9**

YAYA'S BAKERY

One of New York City's last remaining elevated trains runs through the neighborhood of Astoria, Queens. Astoria is home to the Steinway Piano Factory, the old Silvercup Bread Factory (now a film and television studio), and if you've read *The Great Gatsby* you'll remember that Daisy and Tom Buchanan passed through here on their way to East Egg. But these days Astoria is primarily known as Athens West, and YaYa's Bakery does look as if it belongs in a Greek village rather than under the screeching train.

YaYa's is tiny, hot, crowded, and noisy. Three ovens, one of them wood burning, run at high temperatures night and day. The owners and customers shout at one another in Greek, and it will be difficult to find room to turn around, or even move. Meanwhile, the train overhead sounds like a steel mill operating at full power. So what's the attraction? YaYa's traditional Greek pastries are very good, but what holds this bakery aloft is its bread (be sure to try the bread sticks and the sesame seed–laden koulouri rings), which is always just minutes out of the oven that sits three feet away from the display case. YaYa's traditional Greek bread is worth all the tumult. **10**

STATEN ISLAND

Staten Island lays claim to strong historical ties to food. The Pig Wars, a livestock dispute between Native Americans and European settlers, destroyed the island's first settlement in 1641. Staten Island was later settled successfully by freed slaves from Maryland and Virginia who had moved north to transfer their expertise in oyster harvesting to the rich estuaries of New York Harbor.

New York City's relationship with its "forgotten borough" has always been tenuous. For a short period, Staten Island was part of New Jersey, and during New York's financial crisis in the 1970s city legislators seriously considering selling it back to the Garden State. For their part many Staten Islanders, tired of paying taxes for services they did not get, seriously considered secession. In 2013, Staten Island was the borough most impacted by Hurricane Sandy.

While Staten Island is New York's third largest borough, it remains the least populous, with a feeling that is more suburban than urban; you should plan to visit by car. When it comes to food, the emphasis is heavily southern Italian, but you will also find a Russian supermarket and a great Thai store.

Getting to Staten Island can be a lot of fun if you take the Staten Island Ferry: The five-mile, twenty-five-minute trip provides a remarkable view of New York Harbor, and the absence of a fare (the ride is free!) makes the ferry the best bargain in New York. Alternatively, you can depart from Brooklyn and traverse the magnificent Verrazano-Narrows Bridge, which spans Gravesend Bay at the bottom of the harbor. If you make the effort to get to Staten Island, you'll be glad New York held on to its youngest borough.

THE CAKE CHEF'S COOKIE JAR

We loved the Cookie Jar instantly—from the large sign outside the front door to the meticulously arranged wall of cookie jars, and last but not least, the smell of baking cookies permeating the air. If you are a hopeless romantic and have fond memories of your grandmother's cookies, then this is the perfect place for you! There is a revolving roster of more than 150 cookie choices made in small batches. These may include caramel oatmeal squares, Greek nut balls, homemade Oreos, hazelnut stars, coconut brownie bites, almond macaroons, elephant ears, peanut butter and jelly sandwich cookies, and red velvet whoopie pies . . . and some of the cookies are gluten free. You're sure to find beloved classics, as well as new favorites. But for you cookie monsters out there, don't fret if you can't make the trek: All you have to do is visit the website, cakechefcookiejar.com; the Cake Chef will ship anywhere. **2**

BARI PORK STORE

Three generations of the Buttaro family greeted us as we entered the Bari Pork Store. The store flies more flags than Yankee Stadium, with a separate flag for each of the fruits and vegetables sold there. The Bari logo—two pigs fighting over a length of sausage—is everywhere. After tasting Bari's products, we agree: The pork sausage, freshly made mozzarella, and pizza are well worth the trip to Staten Island. However, if you live in Brooklyn, you can visit the store in Bensonhurst. Rumor has it that if you don't get there early, though, the shop will sell out! **1**

PASTOSA RAVIOLI

In 2014, Pastosa Ravioli transformed itself into something akin to the Dean & DeLuca of Staten Island. Vincent d'Antonio and his two sons, Michael and Vincent, changed the look of Pastosa, and it is now a spacious store offering virtually any Italian dish you can think of, all made in a beautiful new kitchen housed in the old store next door. The prepared dishes include spaghetti and meatballs, veal, chicken and eggplant parmigiana, cheese ravioli, lasagna, and many other tempting dishes. The Pastosa family started the cheese and ravioli business in 1894. Unlike other Italian groceries, which stock a variety of different brands, just about every food product in the store carries the Pastosa name.

Our favorite item is the burrata, a cow's milk mozzarella filled with heavy cream that oozes when the cheese is cut, especially when it's served warm as it is at Pastosa. The Italian wedding soup is also one of Pastosa's classics and, of course, all the fresh pasta is not to be missed. Our favorite prepared pasta is the pasta e fagioli, a humble dish of pasta and beans that is delicious. D'Antonio will welcome you as if you are part of the family (and he knows all his regular customers by first name), so you're sure to feel at home as you stroll through the store finding pasta, olive oil, fresh fish, fresh meat, and prepared foods, all sporting detailed hand-lettered descriptions. He even invited us into the kitchen to show us how he makes chicken rollatini. Every time we tried to leave, he offered us a taste of something wonderful. You can only imagine how long we were there! **3**

PHIL-AM FOOD

Behind the green awning above an almost unnoticeable facade, Phil-Am is one of the only groceries and prepared food stores that caters to Staten Island's Filipino community. Phil-Am Food is a family-run business. The father and son team gave us a charming and informative overview of all the different foods sold in the store. They offer a huge array of Filipino packaged foods (try the banana ketchup, the Filipino equivalent of our tomato ketchup), and a small kitchen in the back produces many prepared food options, made fresh daily. These dishes include home-style favorites such as chop suey, ginataan, binagoongan pork, bihon and canton noodles, and kare-kare beef. And the packaged candies, cookies, chips, nuts, and drinks are a visual feast. Don't worry if you can't read the labels: The proprietors will be happy to tell you what is inside every package. **4**

RALPH'S FAMOUS ITALIAN ICES

Since Ralph Silvestro opened this store in 1928, folks from Manhattan, Brooklyn, and New Jersey have come to Ralph's to "have an Italian ice." Although there are now more than seventy-five Ralph's locations in the tristate area, the original Staten Island store is still going strong, and even survived Hurricane Sandy. The facade appears as if it has not been touched since the 1950s, and that's part of its charm. In Italy the closet thing to an "ice" is granita. The Americanized version at Ralph's is denser and packs considerably more flavor and sugar into each scoop. Among the specialties are the margarita ice, which, we were told, mixes well with tequila, and the Ralphiccino, a blend of cappuccino ice with chocolate and 1-percent milk, topped with whipped cream and cinnamon. But at any given time, the store offers up to thirty-six flavors of ices and just about as many choices of sherbet. Arrive early on hot summer days, because the line can extend around the block! **5**

ROYAL CROWN BAKERY

Royal Crown Bakery could have doubled as a location for *The Sopranos*. White plastic chairs and tables are filled to capacity in front of this Italian sidewalk café every day, especially since the shop added a new prepared food section. The food is all homemade from the freshest ingredients. You will understand why this bakery is packed as soon as you taste the rich cappuccino—its foam is thick enough to suspend a large spoonful of sugar. Buy one of the crispy loaves of bread—they are some of the best we have tasted anywhere in New York; we especially recommend the olive, prosciutto, and chocolate loaves. You should also be sure to pick up a jar of the signature Royal Crown balsamic glaze. The bakery says it flies off the shelves, and after trying some, we definitely agree it is a must! **6**

INDEX OF ADDRESSES

NOTE: Only main addresses are listed.
Call or check online for other locations.

BREADS BAKERY, 103
18 East 16th Street
New York, NY 10003
212.633.2253
breadsbakery.com

BRIGHTON BAZAAR, 147
1007 Brighton Beach Avenue
Brooklyn, NY 11235
718.769.1700

THE BROOKLYN KITCHEN, 164
100 Frost Street
Brooklyn, NY 11211
718.389.2982
thebrooklynkitchen.com

**BROOKLYN ROASTING
COMPANY, 150**
25 Jay Street
Brooklyn, NY 11201
718.855.1000
brooklynroasting.com

BURGUNDY WINE, 79
143 West 26th Street
New York, NY 10001
212.691.9092
burgundywinecompany.com

CACAO PRIETO, 160
218 Conover Street
Brooklyn, NY 11231
347.225.0130
cacoprieto.com

**THE CAKE CHEF'S COOKIE
JAR, 180**
1226 Forest Avenue
Staten Island, NY 10310
718.448.3500
cakechefcookiejar.com

CALABRIA PORK STORE, 139
2338 Arthur Avenue,
Bronx, NY 10458
718.367.5145

CALANDRA CHEESE, 139
2314 Arthur Avenue
Bronx, NY 10458
718.365.7572
calandracheese.com

CANELÉ BY CÉLINE, 118
400 East 82nd Street
New York, NY 10028
646.678.4124
canelebyceline.com

**CANTON NOODLE
CORPORATION, 15**
101 Mott Street
New York. NY 10013
212.226.3276

CARRY ON TEA & SYMPATHY, 34
110 Greenwich Avenue
New York, NY 10011
212.989.9735
teaandsympathy.com

CECI-CELA PATISSERIE, 53
55 Spring Street
New York, NY 10002
212.274.9179
ceci-celapatisserie.com

CHELSEA MARKET, 105
75 Ninth Avenue
New York, NY 10011
212.652.2110
chelseamarket.com

Buon Italia
212.633.9090
buonitalia.com

Dickson's Farmstand
212.242.2630
dicksonsfarmstand.com

Doughnuttery
212.633.4359
doughnuttery.com

Eleni's Cookies
212.255.7990
elenis.com

The Lobster Place
212.255.5672
lobsterplace.com

Sarabeth's
212.989.2424
sarabeth.com

**DAMASCUS BREAD & PASTRY
SHOP, 146**
195 Atlantic Avenue
Brooklyn, NY 11201
718.625.7070

DEAN & DELUCA, 90
560 Broadway
New York, NY 10012
212.226.6800
deandeluca.com

DESPAÑA, 53
408 Broome Street
New York, NY 10013
212.219.5050
despanabrandfoods.com

DESPAÑA VINOS Y MAS, 53
410 Broome Street
New York, NY 10013
212.219.1550
despanabrandfoods.com

DI PALO'S FINE FOODS, 55
200 Grand Street
New York, NY 10013
212.226.1033
dipaloselects.com

DOMINIQUE ANSEL BAKERY, 91
189 Spring Street
New York, NY 10012
212.219.2773
dominiqueansel.com

DOUGH, 144
305 Franklin Avenue
Brooklyn, NY 11215
347.533.7544
doughbrooklyn.com

DOUGHNUT PLANT, 61
379 Grand Street
New York, NY 10002
212.505.3700
doughnutplant.com

DOWN TO EARTH MARKET, 157
downtoearthmarket.com
Park Slope: 4th Street at 5th
    Avenue

Calcutta Kitchens
203.434.2317
calcuttakitchens.com

Demi Olive Oil
210.803.8548
demioliveoil.com

Sohha Savory Yogurt
sohhayogurt.com

DYLAN'S CANDY BAR, 118
1011 Third Avenue
New York, NY 10021
646.735.0078
dylanscandybar.com

EATALY, 108
200 Fifth Avenue
New York, NY 10010
212.229.2560
eataly.com

**EAST VILLAGE MEAT MARKET,
26**
139 Second Avenue
New York, NY 10003
212.228.5590
eastvillagemeatmarket.com

ECONOMY CANDY, 61
108 Rivington Street
New York, NY 10002
212.254.1531
economycandy.com

EL TEPEYAC GROCERY, 46
1621 Lexington Avenue
New York, NY 10029
212.987.8364

**ELI'S MARKET AT THE VINEGAR
FACTORY, 119**
431 East 91st Street
New York, NY 10028
212.987.0885

EMPIRE CAKE, 109
112 Eighth Avenue
New York, NY 10011
212.242.5858
empirecake.com

ENOTECA DI PALO, 55
200 Grand Street
New York, NY 10013
212.680.0545

ESPOSITO MEAT MARKET, 80
500 Ninth Avenue
New York, NY 10018
212.279.3298
www.espositomarket.com

ESSEX STREET MARKET, 62
120 Essex Street
New York, NY 10002
essexstreetmarket.com

Ni Japanese Delicacies
646.675.4324

Pain d'Avignon
212.673.4950
paindavignon-nyc.com

Peasant Stock
917.601.9776
facebook.com/
Peasantstockessex

FAICCO'S PORK STORE, 35
260 Bleecker Street
New York, NY 10014
212.243.1974

FAIRWAY, 47
2328 Twelfth Avenue
New York, NY 10027
212.234.3883
fairwaymarket.com

FISH TALES, 148
191 Court Street
Brooklyn, NY 11201
718.246.1346
fishtalesonline.com

FLEISHER'S CRAFT BUTCHERY, 158
192 Fifth Avenue
718.398.6666
Brooklyn, NY 11217
fleishers.com

FLORENCE PRIME MEAT MARKET, 36
5 Jones Street
New York, NY 10014
212.242.6531

FOUR & TWENTY BLACKBIRDS, 150
439 Third Avenue
Brooklyn, NY 11215
718.499.2917
birdsblack.com

FRANÇOIS PAYARD BAKERY, 92
116 West Houston Street
New York, NY 10012
212.995.0888
payard.com

G-FREE NYC, 131
77 West 85th Street
New York, NY 10024
646.781.9770
gfreenyc.com

GASTRONOMIE 491, 131
491 Columbus Avenue
New York, NY 10024
212.974.7871
gastronomie491.com

GEORGETOWN CUPCAKE, 93
111 Mercer Street
New York, NY 10012
212.431.4504
georgetowncupcake.com

GOLDEN PROFIT TRADING, 15
147 Mott Street
New York, NY 10013
212.965.0503

GOOD BEER, 27
422 East 9th Street
New York, NY 10009
212.677.4836
goodbeernyc.com

GOURMET GARAGE, 93
489 Broome Street
New York, NY 10013
212.941.5850
gourmetgarage.com

GRAND CENTRAL MARKET, 80
89 East 42nd Street
New York, NY 10017
grandcentralterminal.com/
market

HARLEM SHAMBLES, 48
2141 Frederick Douglass
Boulevard
New York, NY 10026
646.476.4650
harlemshambles.com

HARNEY & SONS, 94
433 Broome Streeet
New York, NY 10013
212.933.4853
harney.com

HOLYLAND MARKET, 28
122 St. Marks Place
New York, NY 10009
212.477.4440

HUNGARIAN KOSHER CUISINE, 145
5009 16th Avenue
Brooklyn, NY 11204
718.851.0400

IL LABORATORIO DEL GELATO, 66
188 Ludlow Street
New York, NY 10002
212.343.9922
laboratoriodelgelato.com

INTERNATIONAL GROCERY, 82
543 Ninth Avenue
New York, NY 10018
212.279.1000
internationalgrocerynyc.com

INTHIRA THAI MARKET, 173
64-04 39th Avenue
Woodside, NY 11377
718.606.2523

ITALIAN WINE MERCHANTS, 109
108 East 16th Street
New York, NY 10003
212.473.2323
italianwinemerchants.com

JACQUES TORRES, 36
350 Hudson Street
New York, NY 10014
212.414.2450
mrchocolate.com

JAPAN PREMIUM BEEF, 28
57 Great Jones Street
New York, NY 10012
212.260.2333
japanpremiumbeef.com

KALUSTYAN'S, 82
123 Lexington Avenue
New York, NY 10016
212.685.3451
kalustyans.com

KATZ'S DELICATESSEN, 64
205 East Houston Street
New York, NY 10002
212.254.2246
katzsdelicatessen.com

KEE'S CHOCOLATES, 94
80 Thompson Street
New York, NY 10012
212.334.3284
keechocolates.com

KORN'S BAKERY, 146
5004 16th Avenue
Brooklyn, NY 11204
718.851.0268

KOSSAR'S BIALYS, 64
367 Grand Street
New York, NY 10002
212.473.4810
kossars.com

LA BERGAMOTE, 110
177 Ninth Avenue
New York, NY 10019
212.627.9010
labergamotenyc.com

LA BOÎTE, 83
724 11th Avenue
New York, NY 10019
212.247.4407
laboitenyc.com

LADURÉE, 95
398 West Broadway
New York, NY 10012
646.392.7868
laduree.com

LADY M CONFECTIONS, 119
41 East 78th Street
New York, NY 10075
212.452.2222
ladym.com

LE DISTRICT, 73
225 Liberty Street
New York, NY 10286
212.981.8588
ledistrict.com

LE MOULIN À CAFÉ, 121
1439 York Avenue
New York, NY 10075
212.288.5088
lemoulinacafeny.com

LEONARDS' MARKET, 122
1437 Second Avenue
New York, NY 10021
212.744.2600
leonardsnyc.com

LEVAIN BAKERY, 49
2167 Frederick Douglas
    Boulevard
New York, NY 10026
646.455.0952
levainbakery.com

LOBEL'S MEAT, 122
1096 Madison Avenue
New York, NY 10028
212.737.1372
lobels.com

LUCY'S WHEY, 123
1417 Lexington Avenue
New York, NY 10128
212.289.8900
lucywhey.com

LUNG MOON BAKERY, 17
83 Mulberry Street
New York, NY 10013
212.349.4945

MACARON PARLOUR, 29
111 St. Marks Place
New York, NY 10009
212.387.9169
macaronparlour.com

MADONIA BROTHERS BAKERY,
140
2348 Arthur Avenue
Bronx, NY 10458
718.295.5573

MAGNOLIA BAKERY, 37
401 Bleecker Street
New York, NY 10014
212.462.2572
magnoliabakery.com

MAILLE, 132
185 Columbus Avenue
New York, NY 10023
212.724.1014
maile.com

MAISON KAYSER, 124
1294 Third Avenue
New York, NY 10021
212.744.3100
maison-kayser-usa.com

MAKE MY CAKE, 49
121 St. Nicholas Avenue
New York, NY 10026
212.932.0833
makemycake.com

MANSOURA, 156
515 Kings Highway
Brooklyn, NY 11223
718.645.7977
mansoura.com

MARIEBELLE, 96
484 Broome Street
New York, NY 10013
212.925.6999
mariebelle.com

MARK'S WINE & SPIRITS, 17
53 Mott Street
New York, NY 10013
212.962.1993

MARLOW & DAUGHTERS, 163
95 Broadway
Brooklyn, NY 11249
718.388.5700
marlowanddaughters.com

MAST BROTHERS CHOCOLATE,
164
111 North Third Street
New York, NY 11211
718.388.2625
mastbrothers.com

THE MEADOW, 38
523 Hudson Street
New York, NY 10014
212.645.4633
themeadow.com

THE MEAT HOOK, 164
397 Graham Avenue
Brooklyn, NY 11211
718.609.9300
the-meathook.com

MELT, 67
132 Orchard Street
New York, NY 10002
646.535.6358
meltbakery.com

MICHEL CLUIZEL, 84
199 Madison Avenue
New York, NY 10036
646.415.9126
cluizel.us

MINAMOTO KITCHOAN, 84
509 Madison Avenue
New York, NY 10022
212.489.3747
kitchoan.com

MOMOFUKU MILK BAR, 165
382 Metropolitan Avenue
Brooklyn, NY 11211
347.577.9504
milkbarstore.com

MULBERRY MEAT MARKET, 18
89 Mulberry Street
New York, NY 10013
212.267.0350

MURRAY'S CHEESE, 39
254 Bleecker Street
New York, NY 10014
212.243.3289
murrayscheese.com

MURRAY'S STURGEON, 132
2429 Broadway
New York, NY 10024
212.724.2650
murrayssturgeon.com

MYERS OF KESWICK, 41
634 Hudson Street
New York, NY 10014
212.691.4194
myersofkeswick.com

NASSAU MEAT MARKET, 155
915 Manhattan Avenue
Brooklyn, NY 11222
718.389.6149

NEW BEEF KING, 18
89 Bayard Street
New York, NY 10013
212.233.6612
newbeefking.com

NEW KAM MAN, 19
200 Canal Street
New York, NY 10013
212.571.0330
newkamman.com

N.Y. CAKE, 110
55 West 22nd Street
New York, NY 10010
212.675.2253
nycake.com

NEW YORK MART, 20
128 Mott Street
New York, NY 10013
212.680.0178

NUNU CHOCOLATES, 145
529 Atlantic Avenue
Brooklyn, NY 11217
718.834.1818
nunuchocolates.com

O LIVE BROOKLYN, 158
60 Broadway
Brooklyn, NY 11211
718.384.0304
olivebrooklyn.com

OLIVE'S, 97
120 Prince Street
New York, NY 10012
212.941.0111
olivesnyc.com

OMEGA WINES AND SPIRITS,
174
Agora Plaza
23-18 31st Street
Astoria, NY 11105
717.726.0056
omegawinesandspirits.com

ONCE UPON A TART, 98
135 Sullivan Street
New York, NY 10012
212.387.8869
onceuponatart.com

INDEX OF SHOPS BY CATEGORY

Gourmet Garage, 93
Grand Central Market, 80
Le District, 73
New York Mart, 20
Patel Brothers, 174
Sunrise Mart, 30
Sky Foods, 175
Teitel Brothers, 141
Titan Foods, 176
Union Square Greenmarket, 111
Zabar's, 133

FRUITS & VEGETABLES
Agata & Valentina, 116
Arthur Avenue, 136
Asia Market Corporation, 14
Chelsea Market, 105
Dean & Deluca, 90
Down to Earth Market, 157
Eataly, 108
Eli's Market at The Vinegar
    Factory, 119
El Tepeyac Grocery, 46
Fairway, 47
Gourmet Garage, 93
Grand Central Market, 80
Le District, 73
Marlow & Daughters, 163
New York Mart, 20
The Pickle Guys, 67
Produce Stores of Chinatown,
    16
Sky Foods, 175
Subzi Mandi, 175
Teitel Brothers, 141
Union Square Greenmarket, 111
Zabar's, 133

ICE CREAM AND GELATO
Ample Hills Creamery, 159
Babeth's Feast, 117
Il Laboratorio del Gelato, 66
Melt, 67
Popbar, 41
Ralph's Famous Italian Ices, 183

KITCHENWARE
The Brooklyn Kitchen, 164
Eataly, 108
N.Y. Cake, 110
New Kam Man, 19
Zabar's, 133

MEAT, POULTRY, AND GAME
Bari Pork Store, 180

Biancardi Meats, 137
Calabria Pork Store, 139
East Village Meat Market, 26
Esposito & Sons Meat Market,
    80
Faicco's Pork Store, 35
Fleisher's Craft Butchery, 158
Florence Prime Meat Market,
    36
Harlem Shambles, 48
Japan Premium Beef, 28
Leonards' Market, 122
Lobel's Meat, 122
The Meat Hook, 164
Mulberry Meat Market, 18
Nassau Meat Market, 155
New Beef King, 18
Ottomanelli & Sons, 41
Pino's Prime Meat Market, 98
Prime Butcher Baker, 124
Schaller & Weber, 126
Staubitz Market, 149
Stinky Bklyn, 149
Win Sea Market, 22

PASTA
Borgatti's Ravioli & Egg
    Noodles, 138
Calabria Pork Store, 139
Canton Noodle Corporation, 15
Di Palo's, 55
Pastosa Ravioli, 181
Piemonte Ravioli, 56
Raffetto's, 99
Russo's Mozzarella & Pasta, 29

PREPARED FOODS
Agata & Valentina, 116
Babeth's Feast, 117
Barney Greengrass, 130
Chelsea Market, 105
Dean & DeLuca, 90
Eli's Market at The Vinegar
    Factory, 119
Fairway, 47
Gastronomie 491, 131
Gourmet Garage, 93
Grand Central Market, 80
Hungarian Kosher Cuisine, 145
Katz's Delicatessen, 64
Kossar's Bialys, 64
Myers of Keswick, 41
New Beef King, 18
New York Mart, 20

Olive's, 97
Prime Butcher Baker, 124
Petrossian, 85
Russ & Daughters, 68
Sahadi's, 147
Schaller & Weber, 126
William Poll, 127
Yonah Schimmel, 69
Zucker's Bagels & Smoked
    Fish, 75

SEAFOOD
Acme Smoked Fish, 151
Barney Greengrass, 130
Fish Tales, 148
Leonards' Market, 122
Murray's Sturgeon, 132
Randazzo's Seafood, 140
Red Hook Lobster Pound, 161
Russ & Daughters, 68
Sable's Smoked Fish, 126
Win Sea Food Market, 22

TEA AND COFFEE
Bellocq Tea Atelier, 154
Brooklyn Roasting Company,
    150
Carry On Tea & Sympathy, 34
Harney & Sons, 94
Porto Rico Importing
    Company, 42
Sullivan Street Tea & Spice
    Company, 43
Sun's Organic Tea & Herb, 21
Ten Ren Tea, 21
Zabar's, 133

WINES AND SPIRITS
Burgundy Wine, 79
Despaña Vinos Y Mas, 53
Enoteca Di Palo, 55
Good Beer, 27
Italian Wine Merchants, 109
Mark's Wine & Spirits, 17
Omega Wines And Spirits, 174
Pasanella & Son Vitners, 74
Sherry-Lehmann, 127
Wine Therapy, 56

INDEX OF RECIPES